Cooking for One

Kenneth Davies

Help4U Publishing

Copyright © Kenneth Davies 2001.

The right of Kenneth Davies to be identified as the author of this work has been asserted in accordance with the Copyright Designs and Patents Act 1988.

All rights reserved. No part of this publication be may be reproduced, transcribed, transmitted, stored within a retrieval system, translated into another language in any form or by any means electronic, mechanical photocopying, recording or otherwise without the prior permission in writing of the publishers.

A catalogue record of this publication is available from the British Library

First Edition 2001

Although the author has researched the details presented in this book as thoroughly as possible, he assumes no responsibility for any errors, omissions or inaccuracies that may be contained therein. No liability can be accepted for any losses or expenses incurred as a result of relying on any information given therein.

ISBN 1842740199

Internet: www.recipes4one.co.uk

Published by Help4U Publishing, Preston, UK.
http://www.help4u.net
Printed and bound in Great Britain by Antony Rowe Ltd, Eastbourne

Help4U Publishing

Acknowledgments

This book is dedicated to Christine without whom I would never of got started.

I would like to thank Jean and Kevin the proofreaders for their help and support. Not forgetting Ivy and Helen for their help in tasting the many recipes.

Introduction

Cooking for One is a collection of basic recipes that have been created just for one. ***Cooking for One*** is not just for those of us who live alone but also for anyone who needs to cook just a single meal. All the recipes have been designed to use the basic of cooking utensils.

If you wish to try something new or find that others do not have similar tastes or preferences then this book for you. Need a cookbook to give to someone going off to college or university then this will fit the bill.

Like a particular recipes but find there are 2 or more of you no problem just multiply the ingredients by how many of you there are it is that simple. Cooking without kitchen scales all that is needed for these recipes is a set of measuring spoons and measuring cups.

Contents

Appetizers and Soups	3
Breakfasts	45
Main Meals	87
Puddings	129
Snacks and Suppers	171
INDEX	213

Appetizers and Soups

Almond Stuffed Dates with Bacon	5
Antipasto	6
Apple and Cheese Toast	7
Apple & Leek Soup	8
Artichoke Hearts and Parma	9
Avocado Almonds Tempura	10
Avocado Soup	11
Avocado Walnuts & Gloucester Tempura	12
Baby Pineapple Boats	13
Baked French Toast	14
Baked Green & Yellow Pepper Wedges	15
Baked Potato Soup	16
Baked Potato Spears	17
Blue Cheese & Walnut Dip	18
Broccoli & Cheddar Soup	19
Carrot & Orange Soup	20
Carrot & Potato Soup	21
Cauliflower & Broccoli Soup	22
Celery & Green Pepper Soup	23
Celery & Parsnip Soup	24
Cheese & Mushroom Rolls	25
Chicken & Pineapple Salad	26
Chicken & Sweetcorn Soup	27
Crab & Sweetcorn Soup	28

Deep Fried Garlic Mushrooms	29
Feta & Bacon Folded Omelette	30
French Red Onion Soup	31
Fried Brie Cheese	32
Fried Quark Cheese	33
Garlic Croûtons	34
Grapefruit and Stilton Surprise	35
Ham & Pineapple Salad	36
Leek & Potato Soup	37
Minestrone Soup	38
Parma Ham & Galia Melon	39
Potato Skins with Cucumber Dip	40
Potato Skins with Garlic Dip	41
Sauté Prawns & Mushrooms	42
Stilton Cheese Stuffed Bread	43
Vegetable Soup	44

Almond Stuffed Dates with Bacon

8	Whole	Blanched Almonds
8	Pitted	Dates
8	Rashers	Streak Bacon

1. Put an almond in each date.
2. Then wrap a rasher of bacon around each stuffed date and secure with a cocktail stick.
3. Line baking sheet with aluminium foil.
4. Then place the dates on the foil and bake in preheated oven at 350°F, 180°C or Gas Mark 4 oven for 12-15 minutes or until bacon is crisp.
5. Remove from the oven and place on a wire rack or paper towel to drain.
6. Serve at once while still warm.

Antipasto

2	Tablespoon	Extra Virgin Olive Oil
½	Cup	Chopped Carrots
½	Cup	Chopped Red Bell Pepper
½	Cup	Chopped Red Onion
½	Cup	Chopped Cauliflower Florets
½	Cup	Chopped Mushroom
1	Cup	Tined Chopped Tomatoes
½	Cup	Chopped Celery
1	Tablespoon	Tomato Puree
1	Small Tin	Tuna In Oil
1	Pinch	Salt & Pepper

1. Add the olive oil to a medium saucepan and place over a moderate heat.
2. Add the carrots, peppers, cauliflower, mushrooms, celery and onions, sauté for 10 to 15 minutes.
3. Now add the salt, pepper, tomatoes, tomato puree and bring to the boil.
4. Reduce heat and cover, then simmer for 10 to 15 minutes until carrots are tender stirring occasionally.
5. Drain the tuna and add to vegetable mixture, and simmer for 5 minutes longer, letting tuna break up into smaller pieces.
6. Transfer to a warm plate and eat at once.

Apple and Cheese Toast

1	Tablespoon	Butter
1	Medium	Red Eating Apple
½	Teaspoon	Ground Cinnamon
1	Slice	Brown Bread
2	Slices	Edam Cheese

1. Melt butter in a heavy saucepan over a medium heat.
2. Core, quarter and slice the apple.
3. Add ground cinnamon and apple to saucepan and sauté for 4 to 5 minutes.
4. Toast the bread on both sides.
5. Lay the apple slices on the toast and cover with the cheese.
6. Place under a grill for a 3 to 4 minutes until cheese melts.
7. Remove from grill place on a plate and serve at once.

Apple & Leek Soup

2	Medium	Leeks
1	Large	Cooking Apple
1	Tablespoon	Butter
1		Chicken Stock Cube
2	Cups	Water
1	Cup	Apple Juice
1	Teaspoon	Balsamic Vinegar
1	Tablespoon	Calvados or Schnapps
1	Pinch	Salt & Pepper

7. Clean and wash the leeks under running water.
8. Peel and core the apple.
9. Cut both the apple and leeks into thin slices.
10. Melt the butter into a pan over a medium heat.
11. Add the apples, leeks and sauté until just soft.
12. Dissolve the stock cube in the water and add to pan.
13. Add the apple juice, vinegar, calvados, salt and pepper.
14. Bring the liquid to the boil and then reduce to a slow simmer for about 30 to 35 minutes.
15. Ladle soup into a warm bowl and eat at once.

Serving Suggestion
Serve with a fresh bread roll.

Artichoke Hearts and Parma

4	Small	Tined Artichoke Hearts
3	Tablespoon	Extra Virgin Olive Oil
1	Teaspoon	Dried Thyme
1	Teaspoon	Orange Peel
1	Pinch	Black Pepper
4	Slices	Parma Ham, sliced paper thin

1. Wrap each artichoke heart in a slice of Parma ham, secure with a cocktail stick, and place in a deep small dish.
2. In a bowl whisk together the olive oil, thyme, orange peel, and pepper.
3. Pour the dressing over the artichoke hearts and let them marinate in the refrigerator for 1 to 2 hours or overnight.
4. Remove from the refrigerator and serve at room temperature

Avocado Almonds Tempura

2	Small	Chopped Spring Onions
2	Medium	Ripe Avocados, peeled and grated
½	Teaspoon	Ground Coriander
1	Pinch	Salt & Pepper
2	Tablespoons	Lemon Juice
½	Cup	Chopped Almonds
1	Cup	Grated Cheddar Cheese
½	Cup	White SR Flour
1	Medium	Egg
1	Cup	Fresh White Breadcrumbs

1. Place the chopped onions, grated avocados, salt, pepper, coriander and lemon juice in a bowl and mix with a fork.
2. Stir in the chopped nuts and grated cheese the mixture should be firm.
3. Roll the mixture into walnut sized balls.
4. Place the flour in a bowl and dip the ball in it.
5. Beat the egg in a bowl.
6. Then dip the floured balls in the beaten egg and then dip them in the breadcrumbs.
7. Heat a pan of deep oil and cook the balls until they are golden brown all over.
8. Then remove from the pan and place on kitchen paper to drain.
9. Serve at once while they are still hot.

Avocado Soup

1	Small	Avocado
2	Drops	Lime Juice
1		Chicken Stock Cube
2	Cups	Water
1	Teaspoon	Dry Sherry
¼	Cup	Cream
1	Pinch	Salt
1	Pinch	Cayenne Pepper

1. Peel and remove the stone from the avocado.
2. Add avocado and limejuice to a blender and puree it.
3. Mix the chicken stock cube with the water and add to the mixture in the blender and blend for 20 to 30 seconds.
4. Add the sherry to mixture and blend for a few seconds.
5. Pour mixture into a bowl and whisk in cream.
6. Taste and season with the salt and the cayenne pepper.
7. Chill in a refrigerator for at least one hour before and serving.
8. To serve remove from refrigerator and eat at once.

Avocado Walnuts & Gloucester Tempura

2	Small	Chopped Spring Onions
2	Medium	Ripe Avocados, peeled and grated
½	Teaspoon	Ground Coriander
1	Pinch	Salt & Pepper
2	Tablespoons	Lemon Juice
½	Cup	Chopped Walnuts
1	Cup	Grated Double Gloucester Cheese
½	Cup	White SR Flour
1	Medium	Egg
1	Cup	Fresh White Breadcrumbs

1. Place the chopped onions, grated avocados, salt, pepper, coriander and lemon juice in a bowl and mix with a fork.
2. Stir in the chopped nuts and grated cheese the mixture should be firm.
3. Roll the mixture into walnut sized balls.
4. Place the flour in a bowl and dip the ball in it.
5. Beat the egg in a bowl.
6. Then dip the floured balls in the beaten egg and then dip them in the breadcrumbs.
7. Heat a pan of deep oil and cook the balls until they are golden brown all over.
8. Then remove from the pan and place on kitchen paper to drain.
9. Serve at once while they are still hot.

Baby Pineapple Boats

1	Baby	Pineapple
½	Cup	Cottage Cheese
1	Tablespoon	Chopped Walnuts
1	Pinch	Salt & Pepper

1. Cut the baby pineapple in half lengthways leaving the green top on.
2. Remove the pineapple flesh carefully to leave a boat shape.
3. Chop up the pineapple flesh discarding any core.
4. In a bowl mix together the cheese, salt, pepper, walnuts and the chopped pineapple.
5. Spoon the mixture back into one half of the pineapple skins and chill well in a refrigerator before serving.
6. Remove from the refrigerator and eat at once.

Baked French Toast

2	Slices	Whole-Wheat Bread
¼	Cup	Low Fat Milk
1	Medium	Egg
1	Teaspoon	Brown Sugar
2	Drops	Vanilla Extract
1	Pinch	Ground Cinnamon

1. Lightly coat 9"x13"x2" pan with non-stick vegetable spray.
2. Arrange bread slices in bottom of pan.
3. Combine all remaining ingredients and mix well, using whisk or egg beater.
4. Pour mixture evenly over bread.
5. Cover tightly and refrigerate several hours or overnight.
6. Preheat an oven to 350°F, 180°C or Gas Mark 4.
7. Remove bread from refrigerator and spray lightly with non-stick vegetable spray.
8. Bake 30-35 minutes, until lightly browned.
9. Remove from the oven and serve at once.

Baked Green & Yellow Pepper Wedges

2	Medium	Yellow Bell Peppers
2	Medium	Green Bell Peppers
1	Medium	Finely Chopped Onion
1	Small	Tin Chopped Tomatoes
2	Tablespoons	Extra Virgin Olive Oil
2	Cloves	Finely Chopped Garlic
2	Tablespoons	Pine Nuts
½	Cup	Fresh Breadcrumbs
1	Pinch	Salt & Pepper
1	Tablespoon	Chopped Fresh Parsley

1. Preheat oven to 325°F, 190 °C or Gas Mark 5.
2. Lightly oil a baking sheet.
3. Wipe the peppers with damp kitchen paper and then trim tops off peppers; discard stems and finely chop tops.
4. Cut each pepper lengthwise into sixths.
5. Place the wedges, cut side up, in oiled pan and set aside.
6. Mix the pepper tops, onion, tomatoes, parsley, 1 tablespoon olive oil, pine nuts, garlic, salt and pepper in medium size bowl.
7. Spoon equal amounts of mixture into each of the pepper wedges. Bake wedges in preheated oven for 25-30 minutes or until just tender.
8. Sprinkle breadcrumbs and the remaining olive oil over the peppers, and bake for another 10 minutes.

Baked Potato Soup

1	Large	Baking Potato
2	Teaspoons	Butter
2	Tablespoons	Plain White Flour
2	Cups	Milk
1	Pinch	Pepper
3	Medium	Spring Onions, chopped

1. Wash the potato and prick with a fork.
2. Bake the potato in an oven set at 400 °F, 200 °C or Gas Mark 6, for 1 hour or until done.
3. Let it cool then dice the potato and set aside.
4. Melt butter in heavy saucepan.
5. Stir in plain flour and cook for about 1 minute, stirring constantly.
6. Gradually add the milk, stirring constantly until thickened.
7. Bring to a boil add the salt, pepper, diced potatoes and spring onions.
8. Lower the heat and cover, simmer for about 10 minutes.
9. Laddle soup into a warm bowl and eat at once.

Baked Potato Spears

1	Large	Baking Potato
2	Tablespoons	Extra Virgin Olive Oil
1	Pinch	Onion Salt
1	Pinch	Black Pepper

1. Wash and scrub the potato well and cut it lengthwise into thick slices, then cut the slices into thick strips.
2. Brush the strips with the oil.
3. Place on a greased baking sheet and season to taste with the onion salt and pepper.
4. Bake in a moderate oven at 375°F, 190 °C or Gas Mark 5, for 40-50 minutes or until they are tender and golden brown.

Blue Cheese & Walnut Dip

2	Cups	Cream Cheese
1	Tablespoon	Milk
1	Tablespoon	Mayonnaise
1	Tablespoon	Chopped Walnuts
1	Teaspoon	Lemon Juice
1	Teaspoon	Very Finely Minced Onion
½	Teaspoon	Hot Pepper Sauce
½	Teaspoon	Worcestershire Sauce
1	Cup	Grated Blue Cheese

1. Soften the cream cheese in a mixer and gradually beat in the milk to thin it.
2. Add the remaining ingredients and mix well.
3. Place in a small bowl and cover then chill for 1 to 2 hours.
4. Serve slightly chilled or at room temperature

Serving Suggestion
With mixed vegetables cut into matchsticks

Broccoli & Cheddar Soup

1	Teaspoon	Butter
2	Medium	Peeled and Diced Carrots
1	Small	Chopped Onion
1	Cup	Chopped Broccoli
1	Clove	Garlic crushed
1	Medium	Peeled and Diced Potato
¼	Cup	Grated Cheddar Cheese
2	Cups	Warm Water
1		Chicken Stock Cube
1	Pinch	Salt & Pepper

1. Melt butter in a heavy saucepan over a medium heat.
2. Add the diced carrots, chopped onion, broccoli, crushed garlic and diced potato.
3. Cover and cook over low heat for 5 minutes.
4. Mix stock cube with warm water and add to pan.
5. Stir and bring to a boil add salt, pepper.
6. Lower the heat and cover.
7. Simmer for 25 minutes.
8. Just before serving add cheese and let melt.
9. Ladle soup into a warm bowl and eat at once.

Serving Suggestion
Serve hot, delicious with home made croûtons

Carrot & Orange Soup

1	Tablespoons	Butter
2	Medium	Peeled & Diced Carrots
1	Small	Chopped Onion
1	Small	Peeled & Diced Potato
1	Pinch	Salt & Pepper
1	Pinch	Sugar
1	Whole	Vegetable Stock Cube
1	Cup	Warm Water
1	Cup	Orange juice

1. Melt butter in a heavy saucepan over a medium heat.
2. Add the diced carrots, chopped onion, diced potato and sugar.
3. Cover and cook over low heat for 5 minutes.
4. Dissolve the stock in warm water, then add to pan.
5. Stir in the orange juice and bring to a boil, adding the salt and pepper.
6. Lower the heat and cover, simmer for 25 minutes
7. Ladle soup into a warm bowl and eat at once.

Serving Suggestion
Serve hot with home made croûtons.

Carrot & Potato Soup

1	Tablespoons	Butter
2	Medium	Peeled & Diced Carrots
1	Small	Chopped Onion
2	Small	Peeled & Diced Potato
1	Pinch	Salt & Pepper
1	Whole	Vegetable Stock Cube
2	Cups	Warm Water

1. Melt butter in a heavy saucepan over a medium heat.
2. Add the diced carrots, chopped onion and diced potato.
3. Cover and cook over low heat for 5 minutes.
4. Disolve the stock in warm water, then add to pan.
5. Stir and bring to a boil, adding the salt and pepper.
6. Lower the heat and cover, simmer for 25 minutes.
7. Ladle soup into a warm bowl and eat at once.

Serving Suggestion
Serve hot, delicious with home made croûtons.

Cauliflower & Broccoli Soup

1	Cup	Broccoli Florets
1	Cup	Cauliflower Florets
1	Stick	Chopped Celery
1	Small	Diced Potato
1	Small	Chopped Onion
1	Teaspoon	Butter
1	Clove	Garlic Crushed
2	Cups	Warm Water
1		Chicken Stock Cube
1	Pinch	Salt & Pepper

1. Melt butter in a heavy saucepan over a medium heat.
2. Add the broccoli, cauliflower florets, celery chopped onion and diced potato.
3. Cover and cook over low heat for 5 minutes.
4. Mix stock cube with warm water and add to pan.
5. Stir and bring to a boil add salt, pepper.
6. Lower the heat and cover.
7. Simmer for 25 minutes.
8. Ladle soup into a warm bowl and eat at once.

Serving Suggestion
Serve hot with home made croûtons.

Celery & Green Pepper Soup

1	Teaspoon	Butter
2	Cups	Warm water
½	Cup	Milk
2	Sticks	Finely Chopped Celery
1	Small	Chopped Onion
1		Chicken Stock Cube
1	Small	Potato peeled and diced
1	Medium	Diced Green Pepper
1	Pinch	Salt & Pepper

1. Melt butter in a heavy saucepan over a medium heat.
2. Add celery, potato, pepper and onion sauté for 3 to 4 minutes
3. Mix stock cube with warm water and add to pan.
4. Stir and bring to a boil add salt and pepper.
5. Lower the heat and cover and simmer for 20 minutes then add milk.
6. Ladle soup into a warm bowl and eat at once.

Serving Suggestion
Serve at once with thick crusty bread.

Celery & Parsnip Soup

1	Teaspoon	Butter
2	Cups	Warm water
½	Cup	Milk
2	Sticks	Finely Chopped Celery
1	Small	Chopped Onion
1		Chicken Stock Cube
1	Small	Potato peeled and diced
1	Small	Parsnip peeled and diced
1	Pinch	Salt & Pepper

1. Melt butter in a heavy saucepan over a medium heat.
2. Add celery, potato, parsnip and onion sauté for 3 to 4 minutes
3. Mix stock cube with warm water and add to pan.
4. Stir and bring to a boil add salt and pepper.
5. Lower the heat and cover and simmer for 20 minutes then add milk.
6. Ladle soup into a warm bowl and eat at once.

Serving Suggestion
Serve at once with thick crusty bread.

Cheese & Mushroom Rolls

2	Sheets	Filo Pastry
2	Tablespoons	Warmed Extra Virgin Olive Oil
½	Cup	Grated Cheddar Cheese
1	Medium	Chopped Mushroom
1	Teaspoon	Lime Juice
½	Teaspoon	Mixed Herbs

1. Lay out flat one of the sheets of filo pastry and brush with oil then brush the other sheet with oil and place over the top of the first one.
2. Mix together the mushrooms, tomatoes, lime juice and herbs.
3. Place in the middle of the sheets and spread out.
4. Now start at one end and roll up the filo pastry.
5. Transfer to an oiled baking sheet and brush with oil.
6. Bake in a moderate oven at 375°F, 190°C or Gas Mark 5 for 12 to 18 minutes till golden brown.
7. Remove from the oven and serve at once on a warm plate.

Chicken & Pineapple Salad

1	Cup	Diced Cooked Chicken
1	Cup	Mayonnaise with Garlic
1	Small Tin	Pineapple Bits, drained
1	Small Tin	Lychees, drained
2	Sticks	Celery, finely chopped
1	Teaspoon	Clear Honey
¼	Teaspoon	Chilli Powder
½	Bag	Mixed Green Salad

1. In a bowl mix the chicken, pineapple, celery and lychees.
2. Add the mayonnaise, honey, soy sauces, and chilli powder stir well.
3. Check mixed green salad and place on a plate spoon over the chicken mix.
4. Serve with a slice of buttered brown bread.

Chicken & Sweetcorn Soup

1	Small Tin	Sweetcorn
1	Cup	Diced Cooked Chicken
1	Whole	Chicken Stock Cube
2	Cups	Hot Water
2	Tablespoons	Cold Water
1	Teaspoon	Cornflour
1	Teaspoon	Soy Sauce Light
1	Pinch	Salt & Pepper

1. Dissolve the stock cube in the hot water and add to a saucepan.
2. Open and drain the sweetcorn, and chicken and add that to the saucepan with the soy sauce.
3. Place saucepan over a moderate heat and bring to the boil.
4. Blend the cornflour with cold water and add to saucepan.
5. Reduce the heat to low and simmer for 9 to 10 minutes until the soup thickens.
6. Ladle soup into a warm bowl and eat at once.

Serving Suggestion
Serve with a fresh bread roll.

Crab & Sweetcorn Soup

1	Small Tin	Sweetcorn
1	Small Tin	Crabmeat
1	Whole	Fish Stock Cube
2	Cups	Hot Water
2	Tablespoons	Cold Water
1	Teaspoon	Cornflour
1	Teaspoon	Soy Sauce Light
1	Pinch	Salt & Pepper

1. Dissolve the stock cube in the hot water and add to a saucepan.
2. Open and drain the sweetcorn and crabmeat, add these to the saucepan with the soy sauce.
3. Place saucepan over a moderate heat and bring to the boil.
4. Blend the cornflour with cold water and add to saucepan.
5. Reduce the heat to low and simmer for 9 to 10 minutes until the soup thickens.
6. Ladle soup into a warm bowl and eat at once.

Serving Suggestion
Serve with a fresh bread roll.

Deep Fried Garlic Mushrooms

10		Button Mushrooms
3	Cloves	Garlic, crushed
1	Cup	Flour
1	Large	Egg
1	Cup	Fresh Breadcrumbs
1	Tablespoon	Butter

1. Clean mushrooms with damp paper towel.
2. In a bowl mix the butter and garlic.
3. Remove any stems from mushrooms and fill with the butter mix.
4. Then coat with flour shaking off any excess.
5. In a flat dish mix together the breadcrumbs and all the seasonings.
6. Beat the eggs and place in a separate bowl.
7. Dip all the floured mushrooms in the egg and then in the breadcrumbs.
8. Rest in the refrigerator for 30 minutes.
9. Deep fry the coated mushrooms in oil for about 3 to 4 minutes until the coating is cooked

Feta & Bacon Folded Omelette

1	Tablespoon	Butter
2	Medium	Eggs
1	Tablespoon	Milk
½	Cup	Chopped Feta Cheese
2	Rashers	Chopped Bacon
1	Pinch	Salt & Pepper

1. Melt butter in an omelette pan over medium heat, tilting pan to coat bottom and sides.
2. Combine eggs, milk, salt and pepper.
3. Increase heat from medium to high.
4. Pour egg mixture into the omelette pan.
5. Stir only once and cook until edges begin to set.
6. Using a palette knife, gently pull the edges of the egg mixture away from the sides of the pan so that the uncooked portion flows under the cooked edges.
7. Continue until most of the egg mixture is set but the surface of the omelette is slightly wet.
8. Sprinkle the cheese and bacon over the top of the omelette.
9. Fold in half and cook for about 1 minute only until egg mixture is completely set.
10. Tip onto a warm plate and serve immediately.

French Red Onion Soup

1	Large	Red Onion, sliced into rings
2	Teaspoons	Butter
1	Pinch	Salt & Pepper
1	Teaspoon	Worcestershire Sauce
1		Beef Stock Cube
¼	Cup	Red Wine
2	Cups	Water
1	Clove	Garlic, crushed
1		French Bread, thickly sliced
1	Tablespoon	Mozzarella Cheese, grated
1	Teaspoon	Parmesan Cheese

1. Melt the butter in a pan over a medium heat add the onions cover and sauté for 15 to 18 minutes until soft.
2. Remove the cover stir well then increase the heat.
3. Let the onions caramelise keep stirring to stop them burning for about 20 to 25 minutes.
4. Dissolve the stock cube in the water.
5. Add the stock, wine, worcestershire sauce salt and pepper.
6. Bring the liquid the boil and then cover and reduce to a slow simmer for about 15 to 20 minutes.
7. Place bread on a baking sheet in a bake at 275°F, 140°C or Gas Mark 1 for 20 to 25 minutes.
8. Ladle soup into heatproof bowl place bread on top and sprinkle with cheese then place under a grill until cheese is melted serve at once.

Fried Brie Cheese

1	Cup	Brie Cheese, cut into chip size pieces
2	Cups	Breadcrumbs
2	Cups	Flour
1	Large	Egg
1	Teaspoon	Garlic Powder
1	Teaspoon	Oregano
1	Teaspoon	Ground Cumin
1	Pinch	Salt & Pepper

1. Coat cheese pieces with flour shaking off any excess.
2. In a flat dish mix together the breadcrumbs and all the seasonings.
3. Beat the eggs and place in a separate bowl.
4. Dip all the floured cheese in the egg and then in the breadcrumbs.
5. Deep fry the coated cheese in oil for about 3 to 4 minutes until the coating is cooked.

Fried Quark Cheese

1	Cup	Quark Cheese, cut into chip size pieces
2	Cups	Breadcrumbs
2	Cups	Flour
1	Large	Egg
1	Teaspoon	Garlic Powder
1	Teaspoon	Oregano
1	Teaspoon	Ground Cumin
1	Pinch	Salt & Pepper

1. Coat cheese pieces with flour shaking off any excess.
2. In a flat dish mix together the breadcrumbs and all the seasonings.
3. Beat the eggs and place in a separate bowl.
4. Dip all the floured cheese in the egg and then in the breadcrumbs.
5. Deep fry the coated cheese in oil for about 3 to 4 minutes until the coating is cooked.

Garlic Croûtons

1	Slice	White Bread, diced
1	Large	Plastic Food Bag
1	Teaspoon	Garlic Powder
1	Tablespoons	Virgin Olive Oil

1. Preheat an oven to 200°C, 400° F or Gas Mark 6.
2. Place diced bread in the plastic bag add garlic powder close top and shake well.
3. Open bag and add the oil close top and shake well.
4. Empty on to a baking sheet and place in the oven cook for 8 to 9 minutes then remove.

Grapefruit and Stilton Surprise

1	Medium	Grapefruit
1	Tablespoon	Sugar
1	Tablespoon	Port
1	Cup	Stilton, crumbled

1. Cut grapefruit in half loosen segments with a knife and remove any pips.
2. Place in a ovenproof dish sprinkle with sugar, and the cheese pour the port over it.
3. Place under a hot grill for a few minutes until the cheese melts and turns brown.

Ham & Pineapple Salad

1	Cup	Diced Cooked Ham
1	Cup	Mayonnaise with Garlic
1	Small Tin	Pineapple Bits, drained
1	Small Tin	Lychees, drained
2	Sticks	Celery, finely chopped
1	Teaspoon	Clear Honey
¼	Teaspoon	Chilli Powder
½	Bag	Mixed Green Salad

1. In a bowl mix the Ham, pineapple, celery and lychees.
2. Add the mayonnaise, honey and chilli powder stir well.
3. Check mixed green salad and place on a plate spoon over the ham mix.
4. Serve with a slice of buttered brown bread.

Leek & Potato Soup

1	Large	Potato, diced
2	Medium	Leeks, sliced
1	Teaspoon	Butter
1		Vegetable Stock Cube
2	Cups	Water
1	Pinch	Salt & Pepper

1. Clean and wash the leeks under running water.
2. Peel the potatoes and dice them.
3. Cut leeks into thin slices.
4. Melt the butter in a pan over a medium heat.
5. Add the leeks and sauté for 4 to 5 minutes until just soft.
6. Dissolve the stock cube in the water.
7. Add the stock, potatoes, salt and pepper.
8. Bring the liquid to the boil and then cover and reduce to a slow simmer for about 15 to 20 minutes.
9. Ladle soup into a warm bowl and eat at once.

Serving Suggestion
Serve with a fresh bread roll.

Minestrone Soup

1	Tablespoon	Olive Oil
2	Cloves	Garlic, grated
1	Small	Onion, chopped
1	Teaspoon	Tomato Paste
1		Beef Stock Cube
2	Cups	Water
½	Cup	Cabbage, shredded
1	Small	Carrot, sliced
¼	Cup	Macaroni
1	Tin	Tomatoes, chopped
½	Cup	Frozen Green Beans
½	Can	Red Kidney Beans
1	Pinch	Salt
1	Pinch	Black Pepper
1	Pinch	Ground Sage

1. In a large soup pot, sauté garlic, onion until soft.
2. Stir in tomato paste, stock cube, water, cabbage, carrots, salt, pepper and sage.
3. Mix well and bring to a boil. Lower heat, cover and simmer slowly 1 hour.
4. Add remaining ingredients.
5. Cook 10-12 minutes until macaroni is tender.
6. Ladle soup into a warm bowl and sprinkle with Parmesan cheese immediately before serving.

Serving Suggestion
Serve with a fresh bread roll.

Parma Ham & Galia Melon

1	Small	Galia Melon
1	Tablespoon	Lime Juices
4	Slices	Very Thin Parma Ham

1. Cut the melon in half remove the seeds and scoop out melon into balls.
2. Sprinkle with lime juice and allow to stand for 10-30 minutes
3. Cut parma ham into thin strips.
4. Wrap the strips of ham.around the melon balls and fasten with a cocktail stick.
5. Arrange onto a serving platter and serve slightly chilled.

Potato Skins with Cucumber Dip

1	Medium	Baking Potato
½	Cup	Natural Yoghurt
½	Cup	Cucumber, peeled and grated
1	Clove	Garlic, crushed
1	Pinch	Salt & Black Pepper
1	Teaspoon	Chives

1. Preheat oven to 400°F, 200 °C or Gas Mark 6
2. Wash potato and cook for about 40 minutes or until cooked.
3. When cooked halve baked potato lengthwise and scoop out pulp, leaving some pulp attached to skin try to avoid breaking the skin.
4. Cut potato skins into quarters and place on grill skin-sides down grill for 5 minutes or until crisp.
5. Place cucumber in a clean tea towel and squeeze to extract some of the moisture.
6. Add to a large bowl and add all the other ingredients
7. Place in a ramekin dish and serve with potato skins

Potato Skins with Garlic Dip

1	Medium	Baking Potato
2	Cloves	Garlic
2	Small	Spring Onions
¼	Cup	Cream Cheese
1	Tablespoon	Mayonnaise
¼	Cup	Natural Yoghurt
1	Teaspoon	Lime Juice

1. Preheat oven to 400°F, 200°C or Gas Mark 6
2. Wash potato and cook for about 40 minutes or until cooked.
3. When cooked halve baked potato lengthwise and scoop out pulp, leaving some pulp attached to skin try to avoid breaking the skin.
4. Cut potato skins into quarters and place on grill skin-sides down grill for 5 minutes or until crisp.
5. Place the garlic and onions in a food processor then process until it is minced about 1 minute.
6. Add the cheese, yoghurt and mayonnaise and process until smooth.
7. Add the limejuice; pulse 2 to 3 times or until well blended.
8. Spoon into a ramekin dish and cover then chill until needed then serve with potato skins.

Sauté Prawns & Mushrooms

1	Tablespoons	Butter.
2	Cloves	Garlic, crushed.
1	Cup	Mushroom, chopped.
1	Cup	Prawns, cooked.
1	Slice	White Bread
1	Pinch	Paprika

1. Place a frying pan over a moderate heat, add the butter and melt it.
2. Add the crushed garlic and mushrooms to the frying pan and sauté for 3 to 4 minutes.
3. Remove the crusts from the slice of white bread and roll it flat with a rolling pin.
4. Toast the bread on both sides until it is a light golden colour.
5. Add the prawns to the frying pan and stirring well for 1 to 2 minutes just to warm the prawns through.
6. Place the toasted bread on a warm plate and top with the prawns and garlic mixture then sprinkle with paprika.

Stilton Cheese Stuffed Bread

1		Baguette
2	Cups	Grated Stilton Cheese
1	Tablespoon	Butter
1	Teaspoon	Mixed Herbs
1	Tablespoon	Green Onions

1. With curved fruit knife, remove centre from loaf of bread in one piece, leaving 1-inch shell, set shell and centre aside.
2. In large bowl, combine cheese, butter, herbs and onion and toss to mix thoroughly.
3. Spoon about ½ mixture in bottom of bread shell.
4. Using serrated bread knife carefully cut reserved centre of bread into 2-inch squares, keeping shape intact.
5. Replace in bread shell.
6. Press remaining cheese into all openings between pieces.
7. Place on baking sheet and heat in a moderate oven at 350°F, 180°C or Gas Mark 4 for 15 minutes or until cheese melts.
8. Remove from the oven and slice while still warm and eat at once.

Vegetable Soup

1	Teaspoon	Butter
1	Small	Tin Tomatoes, chopped
1	Medium	Carrots, peeled and diced
1	Small	Onion, chopped
1	Small	Potato, peeled and diced
1	Pinch	Salt & Pepper
1	Pinch	Sugar
1		Vegetable Stock Cube
2	Cups	Warm Water

1. Melt butter in a heavy saucepan over a medium heat.
2. Add carrots, potato and onion sauté for 3 to 4 minutes
3. Mix stock cube with warm water and add to pan.
4. Stir and bring to a boil add tomatoes salt and pepper.
5. Lower the heat and cover and simmer for 16 minutes.

Serving Suggestion
Serve at once with thick crusty bread.

Breakfasts

A Toasted Breakfast	47
Bacon & Cheese Bagel	48
Bacon & Cheese Cheese-Crumpet	49
Bacon & Cheese Croissant	50
Bacon & Cheese with Garlic Croissant	51
Bacon & Cheese with Ham Bagel	52
Bacon & Cheese with Herbs Croissant	53
Bacon Folded Omelette	54
Baked Eggs with Ham & Potato	55
Banana & Pear Breakfast Shake	56
Banana Breakfast Shake	57
Breakfast Apple & Banana Bars	58
Breakfast Apple & Walnut Bars	59
Breakfast Apple Bars	60
Breakfast Banana & Walnut Bars	61
Breakfast Cherry Bars	62
Cream Cheese Omelette with Tomato	63
Eggs Florentine	64
French Toast	65
Gloucester Stuffed Bread	66
Grapefruit Surprise	67
Hot Scrambled Eggs	68
Jugged Kipper	69
Malt French Toast	70

Mozzarella & Bacon Folded Omelette	71
Parma Ham & Pineapple	72
Pear & Cheese Toast	73
Pink Grapefruit Surprise	74
Ploughmen's Breakfast	75
Prawns on Toast	76
Prosciutto Ham & Mixed Fruit	77
Quick Kedgeree	78
Scottish Rarebit	79
Scrambled Egg Pockets	80
Smoked Haddock on Toast	81
The Complete Breakfast	82
Tomato Folded Omelette	83
Turkey & Cheese Croissant	84
Walnut French Toast	85
Whole-Wheat French Toast	86

A Toasted Breakfast

1	Slice	Whole-Wheat Bread, toasted
1	Teaspoon	Low Fat Spread
3	Medium	Sliced Mushrooms
1	Medium	Sliced Tomato
1	Rasher	Rind less Bacon, cooked and chopped
2	Tablespoon	Grated Cheese

1. Spread the toast with the low fat spread and place on a baking sheet.
2. Cover with layers of mushrooms and tomato slices.
3. Sprinkle cheese and bacon on top.
4. Place under the grill until the cheese melts.

Bacon & Cheese Bagel

1	Rasher	Bacon
1	medium	Garlic Bagel
1	Slice	Cheddar Cheese

1. Grill the rasher of bacon until it is cooked.
2. Warm the bagel and cut in half leaving a hinged side.
3. Place cooked bacon on one side and the sliced cheese on the other.
4. Return to grill until the cheese is just melting and bagel is only lightly toasted then close and eat at once.

Bacon & Cheese Cheese-Crumpet

1	Rasher	Bacon
1	Medium	Cheese-Crumpet
1	Slice	Cheddar Cheese

1. Grill the rasher of bacon until it is cooked.
2. Warm the crumpet and cut in half leaving a hinged side.
3. Place cooked bacon on one side and the sliced cheese on the other.
4. Return to grill until the cheese is just melting and crumpet is only lightly toasted then close and eat at once.

Bacon & Cheese Croissant

1	Rasher	Bacon
1	Medium	Croissant
1	Slice	Cheddar Cheese

1. Grill the rasher of bacon until it is cooked.
2. Warm the croissant and cut in half leaving a hinged side.
3. Place cooked bacon on one side and the sliced cheese on the other.
4. Return to grill until the cheese is just melting and croissant is only lightly toasted then close and eat at once.

Bacon & Cheese with Garlic Croissant

1	Rasher	Bacon
1	Medium	Croissant
2	Tablespoon	Low Fat Soft Cheese with Garlic

1. Grill the rasher of bacon until it is cooked.
2. Cut the croissant in half leaving a hinged side.
3. Toast croissant until it is a light golden brown.
4. Place cooked bacon on one side and spread the low fat soft cheese with garlic on the other, close and eat at once.

Bacon & Cheese with Ham Bagel

1	Rasher	Bacon
1	Medium	Garlic Bagel
2	Tablespoon	Low Fat Soft Cheese with Ham

1. Grill the rasher of bacon until it is cooked.
2. Cut the bagel in half leaving a hinged side.
3. Toast bagel until it is a light golden brown.
4. Place cooked bacon on one side and spread the low fat soft cheese with ham on the other, close and eat at once.

Bacon & Cheese with Herbs Croissant

1	Rasher	Bacon
1	Medium	Croissant
2	Tablespoon	Low Fat Soft Cheese with Herbs

1. Grill the rasher of bacon until it is cooked.
2. Cut the croissant in half leaving a hinged side.
3. Toast croissant until it is a light golden brown.
4. Place cooked bacon on one side and spread the low fat soft cheese with herbs on the other, close and eat at once.

Bacon Folded Omelette

1	Tablespoons	Butter
2	Medium	Eggs
1	Tablespoons	Milk
2	Rashers	Chopped Bacon
1	Pinch	Salt & Pepper

1. Melt butter in an omelette pan over medium heat, tilting pan to coat bottom and sides with the melted butter.
2. Combine eggs, milk, salt and pepper.
3. Increase heat from medium to high.
4. Pour egg mixture into the omelette pan.
5. Stir only once and cook until edges begin to set.
6. Using a palette knife, gently pull the edges of the egg mixture away from the sides of the pan so that the uncooked portion flows under the cooked edges.
7. Continue until most of the egg mixture is set but the surface of the omelette is slightly wet.
8. Sprinkle the bacon over the top of the omelette.
9. Fold in half and cook for about 1 minute only until egg mixture is completely set.
10. Tip onto a warm plate and serve immediately.

Baked Eggs with Ham & Potato

1	Tablespoon	Butter
1	Small	Onion
1	Cup	Cooked Cubed Potato
½	Cup	Cooked cubed Ham
½	Cup	Cheese
2	Dashes	Worcestershire Sauce
1	Pinch	Salt & Pepper
1	Large	Egg

1. Place a saucepan over a moderate heat and add butter and melt.
2. Peel and thinly slice the onions add to the saucepan then cook until soft, about 5 minutes.
3. Place the cooked onions, cubed cooked potato, ham, cheese, worcestershire sauce, salt and pepper into a bowl and mix well.
4. Butter a small ovenproof dish and add the mixed ingredients.
5. Make a well and carefully break an egg into it.
6. Bake in a moderate oven at 350°F, 180°C or Gas Mark 4 for 15 to 20 minutes until the egg is set.
7. Remove from the oven and eat at once.

Banana & Pear Breakfast Shake

2	Cups	Milk
1	Medium	Banana
1	Medium	Pear
5		Ice Cubes
1	Teaspoon	Wheat germ
3	Drops	Vanilla Extract

1. Peeled and sliced the banana and pear.
2. Combine all the ingredients in a blender container.
3. Blend until smooth, about 20 seconds.

Serving Suggestion
Pour into a glass and drink at once.

Banana Breakfast Shake

2	Cups	Milk
1	Medium	Banana
5		Ice Cubes
1	Teaspoon	Wheat germ
3	Drops	Vanilla Extract

1. Peeled and sliced the banana.
2. Combine all the ingredients in a blender container.
3. Blend until smooth, about 20 seconds.

Serving Suggestion
Pour into a glass and drink at once.

Breakfast Apple & Banana Bars

1	Cup	Whole-Wheat Flour
¾	Cup	White SR Flour
½	Cup	Brown Sugar
1	Cup	Sliced Banana
1	Medium	Eating Apple, grated
½	Cup	Raisins
¼	Cup	Wheat Bran
1	Tablespoon	Baking Powder
½	Teaspoon	Cinnamon
½	Teaspoon	Salt
¼	Teaspoon	Nutmeg
¼	Teaspoon	Baking Soda
¾	Cup	Plain Yoghurt
¼	Cup	Vegetable Oil
2	Medium	Eggs

1. In bowl, mix whole-wheat and SR flours, sugar, sliced banana, raisins, bran, baking powder, cinnamon, salt, nutmeg, grated apple and the baking soda.
2. Whisk together yoghurt, oil and eggs; stir into the dry ingredients.
3. Grease a 9-inch square baking tin and spread the mixed ingredients over the base of the tin evenly
4. Bake in a moderate oven at 350°F, 180°C or Gas Mark 4 for 35 to 40 minutes or when a metal skewer comes out clean after being inserted in the centre of the cooking mix.
5. Remove from the oven and turn out onto a wire rack to cool.
6. Cut into bars.

Breakfast Apple & Walnut Bars

1	Cup	Whole-Wheat Flour
¾	Cup	White SR Flour
½	Cup	Brown Sugar
1	Cup	Chopped Walnuts
1	Medium	Eating Apple, grated
½	Cup	Raisins
¼	Cup	Wheat Bran
1	Tablespoon	Baking Powder
½	Teaspoon	Cinnamon
½	Teaspoon	Salt
¼	Teaspoon	Nutmeg
¼	Teaspoon	Baking Soda
¾	Cup	Plain Yoghurt
¼	Cup	Vegetable Oil
2	Medium	Eggs

1. In bowl, mix whole-wheat and SR flours, sugar, chopped walnuts, raisins, bran, baking powder, cinnamon, salt, nutmeg, grated apple and the baking soda.
2. Whisk together yoghurt, oil and eggs; stir into the dry ingredients.
3. Grease a 9-inch square baking tin and spread the mixed ingredients over the base of the tin evenly
4. Bake in a moderate oven at 350°F, 180°C or Gas Mark 4 for 35 to 40 minutes or when a metal skewer comes out clean after being inserted in the centre of the cooking mix.
5. Remove from the oven and turn out onto a wire rack to cool.
6. Cut into bars.

Breakfast Apple Bars

1	Cup	Whole-Wheat Flour
¾	Cup	White SR Flour
½	Cup	Brown Sugar
½	Cup	Dried Apricots
½	Cup	Chopped Dried Prunes
½	Cup	Raisins
¼	Cup	Wheat Bran
1	Tablespoon	Baking Powder
½	Teaspoon	Cinnamon
½	Teaspoon	Salt
¼	Teaspoon	Nutmeg
¼	Teaspoon	Baking Soda
1	Medium	Eating Apple, grated
¾	Cup	Plain Yoghurt
¼	Cup	Vegetable Oil
2	Medium	Eggs

1. In bowl mix whole-wheat and SR flours, sugar, apricots, prunes, raisins, bran, baking powder, cinnamon, salt, nutmeg, baking soda and the grated apple.
2. Whisk together yoghurt, oil and eggs; stir into the dry ingredients.
3. Grease a 9-inch square baking tin and spread the mixed ingredients over the base of the tin evenly
4. Bake in a moderate oven at 350°F, 180°C or Gas Mark 4 for 35-40 minutes, or when a metal skewer comes out clean after being inserted in the centre of the cooking mix.
5. Remove from the oven and turn out onto a wire rack to cool.
6. Cut into bars.

Breakfast Banana & Walnut Bars

1	Cup	Whole-Wheat Flour
¾	Cup	White SR Flour
½	Cup	Brown Sugar
1	Cup	Sliced Banana
1	Cup	Chopped Walnuts
½	Cup	Raisins
¼	Cup	Wheat Bran
1	Tablespoon	Baking Powder
½	Teaspoon	Cinnamon
½	Teaspoon	Salt
¼	Teaspoon	Nutmeg
¼	Teaspoon	Baking Soda
¾	Cup	Plain Yoghurt
¼	Cup	Vegetable Oil
2	Medium	Eggs

1. In bowl, mix whole-wheat and SR flours, sugar, sliced banana, raisins, bran, baking powder, cinnamon, salt, nutmeg, walnuts and the baking soda.
2. Whisk together yoghurt, oil and eggs; stir into the dry ingredients.
3. Grease a 9-inch square baking tin and spread the mixed ingredients over the base of the tin evenly
4. Bake in a moderate oven at 350°F, 180°C or Gas Mark 4 for 35 to 40 minutes or when a metal skewer comes out clean after being inserted in the centre of the cooking mix.
5. Remove from the oven and turn out onto a wire rack to cool.
6. Cut into bars.

Breakfast Cherry Bars

1	Cup	Whole-Wheat Flour
¾	Cup	White SR Flour
½	Cup	Brown Sugar
½	Cup	Dried Apricots
½	Cup	Chopped Dried Prunes
½	Cup	Raisins
½	Cup	Glace Cherries
¼	Cup	Wheat Bran
1	Tablespoon	Baking Powder
½	Teaspoon	Cinnamon
½	Teaspoon	Salt
¼	Teaspoon	Nutmeg
¼	Teaspoon	Baking Soda
¾	Cup	Plain Yoghurt
¼	Cup	Vegetable Oil
2	Medium	Eggs

1. In bowl mix whole-wheat and SR flours, sugar, apricots, prunes, raisins, bran, baking powder, cinnamon, salt, nutmeg, baking soda and the cherries.
2. Whisk together yoghurt, oil and eggs; stir into the dry ingredients.
3. Grease a 9-inch square baking tin and spread the mixed ingredients over the base of the tin evenly
4. Bake in a moderate oven at 350°F, 180°C or Gas Mark 4 for 35 to 40 minutes or when a metal skewer comes out clean after being inserted in the centre of the cooking mix.
5. Remove from the oven and turn out onto a wire rack to cool.
6. Cut into bars.

Cream Cheese Omelette with Tomato

1	Large	Egg
1	Teaspoon	Cream Cheese
1	Teaspoon	Cream
1	Pinch	Salt & Pepper
1	Tablespoon	Butter
1	Whole	Fresh Tomato, peeled, seeded and chopped

1. Beat egg until light, then beat in cream, salt, and pepper.
2. Melt butter in a frying pan over a moderate heat.
3. Pour egg mixture into frying pan.
4. When starting to set, but still soft, spread tomatoes and cheese over top.
5. Then fold in half and brown on both sides.
6. Remove from pan and serve on a warm plate with oven chips.

Eggs Florentine

1	Cup	Frozen Spinach, chopped
1	Large	Egg
2	Tablespoons	Mayonnaise
1	Tablespoon	Parmesan Cheese, grated

1. Half fill a medium pan with water and put over medium heat bring to the boil.
2. Break the egg into a saucer and slip into boiling water.
3. Reduce the heat so water is just simmering poach for 3 to 4 minutes.
4. Cook spinach according to package directions and then drain thoroughly, place on doubled kitchen paper and squeeze out as much moisture as possible.
5. Butter an ovenproof dish and place the spinach on it.
6. Place the poached eggs on top of spinach and pour mayonnaise over then sprinkle it with cheese.
7. Place under a moderate grill for 5-10 minutes or until top is browned.
8. Serve on a warm plate.

French Toast

1	Cup	Plain Yoghurt
¼	Teaspoon	Vanilla Extract
2	Teaspoon	Sugar
1	Medium	Egg
2	Slices	White Bread
1	Tablespoon	Butter

1. In a small bowl, whisk together the egg, yoghurt, vanilla extract and sugar.
2. Dip the bread into the mixture, coating both sides so as to absorb all the liquid.
3. Place a frying pan over medium and melt the butter.
4. Place the bread into the frying pan and fry until it has browned on both sides.
5. Remove from heat and serve at once.

Gloucester Stuffed Bread

1		Baguette
2	Cups	Grated Double Gloucester Cheese
1	Tablespoon	Butter
1	Teaspoon	Mixed Herbs
1	Tablespoon	Green Onions

1. With curved fruit knife, remove centre from loaf of bread in one piece, leaving 1-inch shell, set shell and centre aside.
2. In large bowl, combine cheese, butter, herbs and onion and toss to mix thoroughly.
3. Spoon about ½ mixture in bottom of bread shell.
4. Using serrated bread knife carefully cut reserved centre of bread into 2-inch squares, keeping shape intact.
5. Replace in bread shell.
6. Press remaining cheese into all openings between pieces.
7. Place on baking sheet and heat in a moderate oven at 350°F, 180 °C or Gas Mark 4 for 15 minutes or until cheese melts.
8. Remove from the oven and slice while still warm and eat at once.

Grapefruit Surprise

1	Medium	Grapefruit
1	Tablespoon	Sugar
1	Tablespoon	Port

1. Cut grapefruit in half loosen segments with a knife and remove any pips.
2. Place one half in an ovenproof dish sprinkle with sugar and pour the port over the top.
3. Place under a hot grill for a few minutes until the sugar melts and turns brown.

Serving Suggestion
Remove and serve at once.

Hot Scrambled Eggs

2	Medium	Eggs
1	Small	Onion, chopped very finely
1	Tablespoon	Butter
1	Teaspoon	Tomato Puree
1	Teaspoon	Curry Powder
1	Slice	Bread

1. Place a pan over a moderate heat add butter and melt add curry powder and onions cook until they are soft, about 10 minutes.
2. Break the eggs into a bowl add the tomato puree and beat.
3. Add egg mix to pan and stir then reduce to a low heat.
4. Stir occasionally until eggs are set.
5. Toast bread under grill and pour eggs on top.

Jugged Kipper

| 1 | Whole | Fresh Kipper |
| 1 | Large Jug | Boiling Water |

1. Place the kipper in a large jug.
2. Pour the boiling water over it so the tail is just uncovered.
3. Leave for 5 minutes then remove.
4. Place on warm plate and top with a knob of butter.

Malt French Toast

1	Cup	Plain Yoghurt
¼	Teaspoon	Vanilla Extract
2	Teaspoon	Sugar
1	Medium	Egg
2	Slices	Malt Bread
1	Tablespoon	Butter

1. In a small bowl, whisk together the egg, yoghurt, vanilla extract and sugar.
2. Dip the bread into the mixture, coating both sides so as to absorb all the liquid.
3. Place a frying pan over medium and melt the butter.
4. Place the bread into the frying pan and fry until it has browned on both sides.
5. Remove from heat and serve at once.

Mozzarella & Bacon Folded Omelette

1	Tablespoons	Butter
2	Medium	Eggs
1	Tablespoons	Milk
½	Cup	Grated Mozzarella
2	Rashers	Chopped Bacon
1	Pinch	Salt & Pepper

1. Melt butter in an omelette pan over medium heat, tilting pan to coat bottom and sides.
2. Combine eggs, milk, salt and pepper.
3. Increase heat from medium to high.
4. Pour egg mixture into the omelette pan.
5. Stir only once and cook until edges begin to set.
6. Using a palette knife, gently pull the edges of the egg mixture away from the sides of the pan so that the uncooked portion flows under the cooked edges.
7. Continue until most of the egg mixture is set but the surface of the omelette is slightly wet.
8. Sprinkle the cheese and bacon over the top of the omelette.
9. Fold in half and cook for about 1 minute only until egg mixture is completely set.
10. Tip onto a warm plate and serve immediately.

Parma Ham & Pineapple

1	Baby	Pineapple
1	Tablespoon	Lime Juice
4	Slices Very Thin Parma Ham	

1. Peel, top and core the pineapple.
2. Cut into chunks.
3. Sprinkle with limejuice and allow to stand for 15 to 20 minutes
4. Cut the parma ham into thin strips
5. Wrap the strips of ham.around the pineapple chunks and fasten with a cocktail stick.
6. Arrange onto a serving platter and serve slightly chilled.

Pear & Cheese Toast

1	Tablespoon	Butter
1	Medium	Eating Pear
½	Teaspoon	Ground Cinnamon
1	Slice	Brown Bread
2	Slices	Edam Cheese

1. Melt butter in a heavy saucepan over a medium heat.
2. Core, quarter and slice the pear
3. Add ground cinnamon and pear slices to saucepan and sauté for 4 to 5 minutes.
4. Toast bread on both sides.
5. Lay pear slices on the toast and cover with cheese.
6. Place under a grill for a 3 to 4 minutes until cheese melts.

Pink Grapefruit Surprise

1	Medium	Pink Grapefruit
1	Tablespoon	Sugar
1	Tablespoon	Port

1. Cut grapefruit in half loosen segments with a knife and remove any pips.
2. Place one half in an ovenproof dish sprinkle with sugar and pour the port over the top.
3. Place under a hot grill for a few minutes until the sugar melts and turns brown.

Serving Suggestion
Remove and serve at once.

Ploughmen's Breakfast

2	Rasher	Chopped Bacon
1	Medium	Cooked Potatoes Cubed
1	Small	Thinly Sliced Onion
1	Small	Egg Beaten
1	Teaspoon	Butter
1	Pinch	Salt & Pepper

1. Heat a frying pan over a moderate heat and melt the butter.
2. Sauté bacon until crisp.
3. Remove from pan, drain on paper towel.
4. Sauté onions in bacon fat until soft.
5. Add potatoes and cook, stirring often, until potatoes start to brown.
6. Add bacon and egg stir constantly until the egg set.
7. Season with salt and pepper to taste.
8. Serve with hot butter toast.

Prawns on Toast

1	Slice	Thick White Bread
½	Cup	Cooked Peeled Prawns
2	Tablespoons	Butter
¼	Teaspoon	Paprika
¼	Teaspoon	Chilli Powder
¼	Teaspoon	Cumin

1. Remove the crust from the bread and roll out with a rolling pin then cut in half length ways.
2. Butter bread on both sides with 1 tablespoon of the butter and place on a baking sheet.
3. Bake in a moderate oven at 350°F, 180°C or Gas Mark 4 for 12 to 14 minutes until golden brown.
4. Melt the other tablespoon of butter in a saucepan over a medium heat; add the prawns and the spices stir well.
5. Heat for 2 to 3 minutes and then spoon on top of the toast.

Prosciutto Ham & Mixed Fruit

2	Small	Fresh Figs
1	Small	Fresh Pear
1	Small	Fresh Peach
4		Seedless Grapes
1	Tablespoon	Lime Juices
4	Slices	Very Thin Prosciutto Ham

1. Peel the figs, pear, and peach.
2. Remove any pits from pear and peach.
3. Cut the fruit into cubes.
4. Combine the figs, pear, peach, and grapes.
5. Sprinkle with limejuice and allow to stand for 10-20 minutes.
6. Cut prosciutto ham into thin strips and wrap around the fruit chunks, then fasten with a cocktail stick.
7. Arrange onto a serving platter and serve slightly chilled.

Quick Kedgeree

½	Cup	Cooked White Rice
½	Cup	Cooked smoked haddock, flaked
1	Medium	Hard Boiled Egg, chopped
1	Tablespoon	Evaporated Milk
1	Tablespoon	Turmeric
½	Teaspoon	Nutmeg, grated

1. Mix all the ingredients in a bowl except the oil.
2. Heat a frying pan over a moderate heat and the oil then empty the bowl into the pan and warm for about 3 to 5 minutes.

Serving Suggestion
Serve on a warm plate

Scottish Rarebit

1	Portion	Finnan Haddock
2	Cups	Milk
1	Tablespoon	Flour
½	Cup	Cheese, grated
1	Medium	Egg
1	Pinch	Salt & Pepper

1. Place a pan of salted water on a moderate heat and bring to the boil.
2. Add fish and cook for 7 minutes.
3. Remove fish and place in an ovenproof dish.
4. Blend the flour with the milk in a bowl.
5. Place a saucepan over a moderate heat and add milk mix, bring to the boil then add half the cheese salt, pepper and the egg.
6. Stir the mixture until sauce thickens about 3 to 4 minutes.
7. Pour over fish and sprinkle the rest of the cheese over it, put under the grill to let cheese brown.

Scrambled Egg Pockets

1	Cup	Tinned Tomatoes, chopped
1	Small	Onion, chopped
1	Small	Green Bell Pepper, chopped
1	Large	Egg
1	Tablespoon	Extra Virgin Olive Oil
1	Teaspoon	Mixed Herbs
1	Pinch	Salt & Pepper
1	Whole	Garlic Pita Bread

1. Make a pocket in the pita bread by cutting down one edge.
2. Heat a fry pan and add oil.
3. Add onions and peppers and sauté for 5 to 6 minutes until softened.
4. Now add, tomatoes to pan and sauté for a further 2 minutes.
5. Then add herbs, salt and pepper to egg and beat then pour into pan and stir until set.
6. Spoon the egg mixture into the pita bread pocket.

Serving Suggestion
Serve at once on a warm plate.

Smoked Haddock on Toast

1	Portion	Finnan Haddock
1	Tablespoon	Butter
1	Cup	Milk
1	Tablespoon	Flour
1	Slice	Bread, toasted
1	Pinch	Salt & Pepper

1. Add the milk and butter to saucepan, place over a moderate heat and add fish and cook for 5 to 6 minutes.
2. Remove fish and flake it into dish removing any bones or skin keep warm.
3. Blend the flour with a little milk taken from the saucepan then add to rest of milk and stir.
4. Bring to a boil add salt, pepper and stir the mixture until sauce thickens about 3 to 4 minutes.
5. Toast the bread and butter it then top with the flaked fish pour sauce over the top and serve.

The Complete Breakfast

1	Slice	Whole-Wheat Bread, toasted
1	Teaspoon	Butter
2	Medium	Fresh Mushrooms, thin sliced
1	Medium	Tomato, thin sliced
1	Tablespoon	Parmesan Cheese, grated
1	Rasher	Smoked Bacon, chopped
1	Dash	Worcestershire Sauce

1. Place toast on baking sheet.
2. Spread with butter if desired.
3. Cover with mushroom and tomato slices.
4. Sprinkle cheese, chopped bacon on top and add a dash of worcestershire sauce.
5. Bake in a moderate oven at 350°F, 180°C or Gas Mark 4 until cheese melts.

Tomato Folded Omelette

1	Tablespoon	Butter
2	Medium	Eggs
1	Tablespoon	Milk
1	Pinch	Salt & Pepper
1	Cup	Chopped Tomatoes

1. Melt butter in an omelette pan over medium heat, tilting pan to coat bottom and sides.
2. Combine eggs, milk, salt and pepper.
3. Increase heat from medium to high.
4. Pour egg mixture into the omelette pan.
5. Stir only once and cook until edges begin to set.
6. Using a palette knife, gently pull the edges of the egg mixture away from the sides of the pan so that the uncooked portion flows under the cooked edges.
7. Continue until most of the egg mixture is set but the surface of the omelette is slightly wet.
8. Sprinkle the tomatoes over the top of the omelette.
9. Fold in half and cook for about 1 minute only until egg mixture is completely set.
10. Tip onto a warm plate and serve immediately.

Turkey & Cheese Croissant

1	Slice	Cooked Turkey
1		Croissant
1	Slice	Cheddar Cheese

1. Warm the croissant and cut in half leaving a hinged side.
2. Place the slice of turkey on one side and the sliced cheese on the other.
3. Return to grill until the cheese is just melting and croissant is only lightly toasted then close and eat.

Walnut French Toast

1	Cup	Plain Yoghurt
¼	Teaspoon	Vanilla Extract
2	Teaspoon	Sugar
1	Medium	Egg
2	Slices	Walnut Bread
1	Tablespoon	Butter

1. In a small bowl, whisk together the egg, yoghurt, vanilla extract and sugar.
2. Dip the bread into the mixture, coating both sides so as to absorb all the liquid.
3. Place a frying pan over medium and melt the butter.
4. Place the bread into the frying pan and fry until it has browned on both sides.
5. Remove from heat and serve at once.

Whole-Wheat French Toast

1	Cup	Plain Yoghurt
¼	Teaspoon	Vanilla Extract
2	Teaspoons	Sugar
1	Medium	Egg
2	Slices	Whole-Wheat Bread
1	Tablespoon	Butter

1. In a small bowl, whisk together the egg, yoghurt, vanilla extract and sugar.
2. Dip the bread into the mixture, coating both sides so as to absorb all the liquid.
3. Place a frying pan over medium and melt the butter.
4. Place the bread into the frying pan and fry until it has browned on both sides.
5. Remove from heat and serve at once.

Main Meals

Barbecue Baby Ribs	89
Barbecue Chicken Drumsticks	90
Barbecue Pork Chop	91
Beef & Mushroom Lasagne	92
Beef & Pineapple Salad	93
Beef Chop Suey	94
Beef Curry	95
Beef Stroganoff	96
Beefsteak with Mushroom & Onion Gravy	97
Bolognese	98
Cajun Chicken Breast	99
Cajun Red Beans & Rice	100
Cheese & Pineapple Pizza	101
Cheese Stuffed Plantains	102
Chicken Chop Suey	103
Chicken Curry	104
Chicken with Mushrooms & Whisky	105
Chinese Folded Omelette	106
Chilli Con Carne	107
Christmas Chestnut Pie	108
Cod Parcels	109
Cod with Cheese Sauce	110
Deep Dish Pineapple & Ham Cheese Pizza	111
Duck with Blackcurrants	112

Duck with Orange	113
Edam Stuffed Brown Pasta Quills	114
Gammon Steak with Pineapple Sauce	115
Goujons Chicken	116
Goujons Turkey	117
Grilled Cod with a Whisky Sauce	118
Grilled Lamb Chop with Mustard	119
Grilled Salmon with a Schnapps Sauce	120
Halibut with Cheese Sauce	121
Italian Lamb Crumble	122
Lamb Hotpot	123
Plaice with Cheese Sauce	124
Prawn Chop Suey	125
Sauté Prawns	126
Steak & Mushroom Pie	127
Steak with Mushrooms & Schnapps	128

Barbecue Baby Ribs

1	Cup	Orange Juice
½	Cup	Peanut Butter
1	Tablespoon	Chilli Pepper Sauce
1	Clove	Garlic, crushed
1	Medium	Rack of Baby Pork Ribs
1	Medium	Sliced Orange

1. Preheat an oven to 375°F, 190°C or Gas Mark 5.
2. In a large bowl combine the peanut butter, garlic, chilli pepper sauce and orange juice.
3. Place the ribs in a shallow baking dish.
4. Coat ribs completely with the mixture.
5. Arrange the slices of orange over ribs.
6. Cover dish with a lid or aluminum foil and bake for 50 to 55 minutes.
7. Uncover dish and bake until juice in dish reduces enough for sauce to stick to the ribs.

Barbecue Chicken Drumsticks

2		Chicken Drumsticks
2	Tablespoons	Brown Sugar
1	Tablespoon	Worcestershire Sauce
2	Cups	Tomato Ketchup
1	Small	Finely Chopped Onion

1. Cut off the small piece from the chicken drumsticks and the bony part so you have only the meaty part left.
2. Mix the ketchup, onion, brown sugar and Worcestershire sauce together.
3. Dip the chicken drumsticks in the sauce.
4. Then place them on an oiled baking sheet.
5. Bake in a moderate oven at 350°F, 180°C or Gas Mark 4 for about 25 to 30 minutes.
6. Warm any remaining sauce in a saucepan and pour over the chicken after you have remove it from the oven

Barbecue Pork Chop

1		Pork Chop
2	Tablespoons	Brown Sugar
1	Tablespoon	Worcestershire Sauce
2	Cups	Tomato Ketchup
1	Small	Finely Chopped Onion

1. Mix the ketchup, onion, brown sugar and Worcestershire sauce together.
2. Dip the pork chop in the sauce.
3. Then place it on an oiled baking sheet.
4. Bake in a moderate oven at 350°F, 180°C or Gas Mark 4 for about 25 to 30 minutes.
5. Warm any remaining sauce in a saucepan and pour over the pork chop after you have remove it from the oven

Beef & Mushroom Lasagne

2	Sheets	No Pre-Cooking Lasagne
1	Small Tin	Chopped Tomatoes,
2	Cups	Lean Minced Beef
2	Cloves	Garlic
1	Small	Onion
1	Cup	Sliced Mushrooms
2	Tablespoons	Grated Mozzarella Cheese
1	Teaspoon	Tomato Puree
1	Teaspoon	Italian Seasoning
1	Tablespoon	Butter
2	Cups	Milk
1	Tablespoon	Cornflour

1. Heat a frying pan over a moderate heat and add the beef stir until meat browns and separates into grains.
2. Peel and finely chop the onion and crush the garlic, add to the frying pan with the tomatoes, mushrooms, puree and seasoning.
3. Bring to the boil then reduce heat and cook for about 14 to 18 minutes until sauce thickens.
4. Put half of the mixture into a shallow ovenproof dish cover with a sheet of lasagne then the remaining sauces and top with a sheet of lasagne.
5. Place a pan over a medium heat, add the butter and melt, add the cornflour and cook for 1 to 2 minutes stirring continually.
6. Slowly add the milk, salt and pepper, stir well, increase the heat, and cook for 4 minutes until sauce thickens.
7. Pour over the top of the last sheet of lasagne and sprinkle with the Mozzarella Cheese.
8. Bake in a moderate oven at 375°F, 190°C or Gas Mark 5 for 25 to 30 minutes until golden brown.

Beef & Pineapple Salad

1	Cup	Diced Cooked Beef
1	Cup	Mayonnaise with Garlic
1	Small Tin	Pineapple Bits, drained
1	Small Tin	Lychees, drained
2	Sticks	Celery, finely chopped
1	Teaspoon	Clear Honey
¼	Teaspoon	Chilli Powder
½	Bag	Mixed Green Salad

1. In a bowl mix the beef, pineapple, celery and lychees.
2. Add the mayonnaise, honey, soy sauces, and chilli powder stir well.
3. Check mixed green salad and place on a plate spoon over the beef mix.
4. Serve with a slice of buttered brown bread.

Beef Chop Suey

1	Tablespoon	Nut Oil
1	Small	Finely Chopped Onion,
1	Small	Finely Chopped Red Pepper
1	Small	Finely Chopped Yellow Pepper
1	Large	Finely Grated Carrot
1	Stick	Finely Chopped Celery
1	Small	Tin Bean Sprouts
2	Cups	Sliced Cooked Beef
1	Teaspoon	Light Soy Sauce
¼		Vegetable Stock Cube
2	Tablespoons	Water

1. Heat a wok or a deep frying pan over a moderate heat add the oil
2. Now add the onion, red pepper, yellow pepper, carrot and celery and stir-fry for 1 to 2 minutes.
3. Add the bean sprouts and beef stir well then add the stock cube, water and soy sauce stir-fry for another 1 to 2 minutes until cooked.

Serving Suggestion
Serve on a bed of rice

Beef Curry

1	Tablespoons	Butter
1	Medium	Onion
1	Clove	Garlic
2	Cups	Cubed Beef
2	Tablespoons	Mild Curry Paste
1	Tablespoon	Coriander
1	Tablespoon	Sultanas
1	Teaspoon	Lime Juice
2	Cups	Natural Yoghurt

1. Heat a saucepan and melt the butter.
2. Peel and chop the onion and crush the garlic.
3. Add beef, garlic and onions to the saucepan and sauté for 10 to 15 minutes.
4. In a bowl mix together the curry paste, yoghurt, lime juice, coriander and sultanas.
5. Pour the yoghurt mixture over the beef and heat gently for 1-2 minutes.
6. When cooked pour on to a warm plate.

Serving Suggestion
Serve with rice or oven chips.

Beef Stroganoff

1	Portion	Beef Fillet Steak
2	Tablespoons	Butter
1	Small	Onion, thinly sliced
1	Cup	Button Mushrooms
1	Tablespoon	Brandy or Schnapps
¼	Cup	Cream
1	Pinch	Salt & Pepper

1. Cut steak into thin strips about an inch long.
2. Heat a fry pan and add 1 tablespoon of the butter.
3. Add onions and sauté for 2 to 3 minutes until softened.
4. Now add mushrooms to pan and sauté them both for a further 2 minutes.
5. Remove from pan now add remaining butter to pan and melt.
6. Add beef and sauté for about 3 to 5 minutes.
7. Now add brandy to beef in pan and ignite shake pan until flames subside.
8. Return mushrooms and onions to pan add salt, pepper and stir in cream.
9. Cook for about 1 minute until all the ingredients are well heated.

Serving Suggestion
To serve pour onto a warm plate and eat at once.

Beefsteak with Mushroom & Onion Gravy

1	Medium	Beefsteak
1	Cup	Sliced Mushrooms
1	Small	Finely Chopped Onion
1	Tablespoon	Extra Virgin Olive Oil
1		Beef Stock Cube
2	Cups	Warm Water
1	Pinch	Salt & Pepper

1. Trim the steak and wipe with kitchen paper.
2. Heat a fry pan and add oil.
3. Add onions and sauté for 2 to 3 minutes until softened.
4. Now add mushrooms to pan and sauté them both for a further 2 minutes.
5. Add steak and sauté for about 3 to 5 minutes.
6. Mix beef stock cube in water add salt, pepper and stir into the pan.
7. Cook for about 25 minute over a moderate heat until and the ingredients thicken.
8. To serve pour onto a warm plate and eat at once.

Bolognese

2	Cups	Lean Minced Beef
1	Small	Finely Chopped Onion
1	Small Tin	Chopped Tomatoes
1	Teaspoon	Tomato Puree
2	Cloves	Garlic
1	Teaspoon	Italian Seasoning
1	Portion	Spaghetti
1	Tablespoon	Parmesan Cheese

1. Heat a frying pan over a moderate heat and add the beef and onions.
2. Crush the garlic and add it to the frying pan, stir until meat browns and separates into grains.
3. Add chopped tomatoes, tomato puree and Italian seasoning.
4. Bring to the boil then reduce heat stiring from time to time.
5. Cook for about 14 to 18 minutes until sauce thickens.
6. Cook the spaghetti according to the directions on the packet.
7. When cooked drain and put on plate spoon the bolognese sauce over it and top with Parmesan cheese.

Cajun Chicken Breast

1	Medium	Chicken Breast
1	Tablespoon	Honey
1	Tablespoon	Cajun Seasoning
1	Cup	Breadcrumbs, fresh
1	Pinch	Salt & Pepper

1. Remove any skin from chicken and wipe with kitchen paper.
2. In a bowl mix together the breadcrumbs and seasoning.
3. Brush the chicken with the honey coating evenly on both sides.
4. Dredge chicken with the breadcrumb mixture.
5. Place chicken on an oiled baking sheet.
6. Bake in a moderate oven at 375 °F, 190 °C or Gas Mark 5 for 20 to 25 minutes until coating is golden brown.
7. Remove from oven and serve with cooked potoes and mixed vegetables

Cajun Red Beans & Rice

1	Cup	Tined Red Kidney Beans
½	Cup	Chopped Onions
1	Teaspoon	Thyme
1	Teaspoon	Parsley
1	Teaspoon	Blackened Cajun Seasoning
2	Cloves	Garlic, crushed
1	Medium	Yellow Bell Pepper
2	Cups	Cooked Brown Rice
3	Cups	Water
1	Pinch	Salt

1. Rinse beans and drain well.
2. Add the water, beans, Cajun seasoning, onion, thyme, garlic, parsley, yellow pepper and salt to a saucepan.
3. Bring to the boil then reduce the heat and simmer over medium heat for 10 to 15 minutes.
4. Then add rice and simmer for another 5 minutes.
5. Serve at once on a warm plate.

Cheese & Pineapple Pizza

1	Cup	White SR Flour
2	Tablespoons	Extra Virgin Olive Oil
1	Tablespoon	Water
1	Teaspoon	Salt
1	Small Tin	Chopped Tomatoes
1	Cup	Grated Cheese
1	Cup	Tinned Pineapple Bits
1	Teaspoon	Italian Seasoning

1. In a bowl, mix the flour, salt, water and oil into a stiff dough.
2. Roll out the dough on a floured surface into a circle.
3. Then place onto a greased baking sheet
4. Heat a pan over moderate heat and add tomatoes and herbs bring to the boil and let boil for 5 to 7 minutes until the sauce has reduced by half.
5. Pour over base and top with pineapples and the cheese.
6. Bake in a moderate oven at 400°F, 200°C or Gas Mark 6 for 15 to 20 minutes until golden brown.
7. Remove from the oven and serve at once.

Cheese Stuffed Plantains

2	Small	Ripe Plantains, unpeeled and halved
4	Cups	Salted Water
2	Tablespoons	Butter
2	Tablespoons	Cornflour
1	Cup	Grated Cheese
1	Pinch	Salt

1. Bring the water to a boil when boiling add the plantains.
2. Cover and boil for 20 minutes.
3. Drain the plantains then peel, mash and combine with butter, salt and cornflour.
4. Let the mixture cool.
5. Coat your hands with cornflour then take some mixture, and form a well in centre and stuff it with the cheese.
6. Cover with more mixture and shape into a ball.
7. Repeat to make 4 balls.
8. Deep fry until golden.
9. Remove and drain on kitchen paper.

Chicken Chop Suey

1	Tablespoon	Nut Oil
1	Small	Finely Chopped Onion,
1	Small	Finely Chopped Red Pepper
1	Small	Finely Chopped Yellow Pepper
1	Large	Finely Grated Carrot
1	Stick	Finely Chopped Celery
1	Small	Tin Bean Sprouts
2	Cups	Sliced Cooked Chicken
1	Teaspoon	Light Soy Sauce
¼		Vegetable Stock Cube
2	Tablespoons	Water

1. Heat a wok or a deep frying pan over a moderate heat add the oil
2. Now add the onion, red pepper, yellow pepper, carrot and celery and stir-fry for 1 to 2 minutes.
3. Add the bean sprouts and chicken stir well then add the stock cube, water and soy sauce stir-fry for another 1 to 2 minutes until cooked.

Serving Suggestion
Serve on a bed of rice

Chicken Curry

1	Medium	Chicken Breast, cubed
1	Medium	Onion, chopped
2	Tablespoons	Butter
1	Clove	Garlic, crushed
2	Tablespoons	Mild Curry Paste
2	Cups	Natural Yoghurt
1	Tablespoon	Coriander
1	Tablespoon	Sultanas
1	Teaspoon	Lime Juice
1	Pinch	Salt & Pepper

1. Heat a saucepan and melt the butter.
2. Add chicken, garlic and onions sauté for 10 to 15 minutes.
3. In a bowl mix together the curry paste, yoghurt, lime juice, coriander, salt, pepper and sultanas.
4. Pour yoghurt mixture over the chicken and heat gently for 1-2 minutes.

Serving Suggestion
Serve with rice.

Chicken with Mushrooms & Whisky

1	Medium	Chicken Breast, boned and skinned
1	Cup	Button Mushrooms
1	Small	Onion, thinly sliced
2	Tablespoons	Butter
1	Tablespoon	Whisky
¼	Cup	Cream
1	Pinch	Salt & Pepper

1. Cut chicken into thin strips about an inch long.
2. Heat a fry pan and add 1 tablespoon of the butter.
3. Add onions and sauté for 2 to 3 minutes until softened.
4. Now add mushrooms to pan and sauté them both for a further 2 minutes.
5. Remove from pan, now add remaining butter to pan and melt.
6. Add chicken and sauté for about 3 to 5 minutes.
7. Now add whisky to chicken in pan and ignite shake pan until flames subside.
8. Return mushrooms and onions to pan and stir in cream.
9. Cook for about 1 minute until and the ingredients are well heated.
10. Serve at once on a warm plate with mixed vegetables.

Chinese Folded Omelette

1	Tablespoons	Butter
2	Medium	Eggs
1	Tablespoons	Milk
1	Pinch	Salt & Pepper
1	Cup	Cooked Prawns
1	Cup	Chinese Mixed Vegetables

1. Melt butter in an omelette pan over a medium heat, tilting pan to coat bottom and sides.
2. Combine eggs, milk, salt and pepper.
3. Increase heat from medium to high.
4. Pour egg mixture into the omelette pan.
5. Stir only once and cook until edges begin to set.
6. Using a palette knife, gently pull the edges of the egg mixture away from the sides of the pan so that the uncooked portion flows under the cooked edges.
7. Continue until most of the egg mixture is set but the surface of the omelette is slightly wet.
8. Sprinkle the prawns and vegetables over the top of the omelette.
9. Fold in half and cook for about 1 minute only until egg mixture is completely set.
10. Tip onto a warm plate and serve immediately.

Chilli Con Carne

2	Cups	Lean Minced Beef
1	Cup	Cooked Red Kidney Beans
1	Small Tin	Tomatoes, chopped
2	Cups	Water
1	Whole	Beef Stock Cube
1	Small	Onion, finely chopped
1	Teaspoon	Tomato Puree
1	Teaspoon	Chilli Powder

1. Heat a frying pan over a moderate heat and add the beef, onions stir until meat browns and separates into grains.
2. Add chopped tomatoes, tomato puree, kidney beans and chilli power.
3. Mix water with stock cube and add to pan.
4. Bring to the boil then cover and reduce heat to a simmer, stir from time to time.
5. Simmer for about 30 to 35 minutes then add the red beans and simmer for another 10 to 15 minutes.

Serving Suggestion
To serve spoon into a warm bowl and serve with crusty bread.

Christmas Chestnut Pie

2	Tablespoons	Butter
1	Small	Onion
1	Cup	Chestnut Mushrooms, sliced
1	Tablespoon	Flour
1	Tablespoon	Double Cream
1	Cup	Water
½	Whole	Vegetable Stock Cube
1	Small	Can Whole Chestnuts, drained and sliced
1	Pack	Ready-made puff pastry
1	Pinch	Salt & Pepper

1. Place a saucepan over a moderate heat and add the butter, onions and mushrooms then sauté for 4 minutes.
2. Add the flour, cream, stock cube and water stir well and bring to the boil and cook for 2 to 3 minutes.
3. Now add the chestnuts, salt and pepper then pour the mixture into a small pie dish.
4. Roll out the pastry and cover the pie, bake at 200°C, 400°F or Gas Mark 6 for 20 minutes.
5. Remove from the oven and eat at once.

Cod Parcels

1	Portion	Cod Fillet
2	Sheets	Filo Pastry
2	Tablespoons	Extra Virgin Olive Oil, warmed
1	Small	Tomato, skinned and chopped
1	Medium	Mushroom, chopped
½	Teaspoon	Mixed Herbs
1	Teaspoon	Lime Juice

1. Lay flat one of the sheets of filo pastry and brush with oil, now brush the other sheet with oil and place over the top of the other one.
2. Mix together the mushrooms, tomatoes, limejuice and herbs
3. Place the cod in the middle of the sheets
4. Spread the mixture over the cod.
5. Now draw up all the sides and squeeze the top together, brush with the oil.
6. Transfer to an oiled baking sheet
7. Bake in a moderate oven at 375°F, 190°C or Gas Mark 5 for 12 to 18 minutes until golden brown.
8. Remove from the oven and serve with a jacket potato and a green salad.

Cod with Cheese Sauce

1	Fillet	Cod
2	Cups	Milk
2	Cloves	Garlic, chopped
2	Tablespoons	Strong Cooking Cheese, grated
2	Tablespoons	Mozzarella Cheese, grated
1	Teaspoon	Italian Seasoning
1	Tablespoon	Butter
1	Tablespoon	Cornflour
1	Pinch	Salt & Pepper

1. Place a saucepan over a medium heat add the butter and melt then add the cornflour and cook for 1 to 2 minutes stirring all the time.
2. Slowly add the milk, salt, pepper, garlic, Italian seasoning and cooking cheese stir well and increase the heat and cook for 4 minutes until sauce thickens.
3. Place the fish into an ovenproof dish pour over the sauce and sprinkle with the mozzarella cheese.
4. Bake in a moderate oven at 375°F, 190°C or Gas Mark 5 for 18 to 20 minutes, until golden brown.
5. Remove from the oven and serve with mashed potatoes and mixed vegetables.

Deep Dish Pineapple & Ham Cheese Pizza

1	Cup	SR Flour
2	Tablespoons	Extra Virgin Olive Oil
1	Tablespoon	Water
1	Teaspoon	Salt
1	Small Tin	Tomatoes, chopped
1	Cup	Mozzarella Cheese, grated
1	Cup	Tinned Pineapple, chopped
1	Cup	Mushrooms, chopped
1	Slice	Cooked Ham, chopped
1	Teaspoon	Italian Seasoning

1. In a bowl mix the flour, salt, water and oil to a stiff dough.
2. Roll out the dough on a floured surface into a circle.
3. Line the base and sides of a greased small Yorkshire pudding tin.
4. Heat a pan over moderate heat and add tomatoes and herbs bring to the boil and let boil for 5 to 7 minutes until the sauce has reduced by half.
5. Pour over base and top with mushrooms, pineapples, ham and the cheese.
6. Bake in a moderate oven at 400°F, 200°C or Gas Mark 6 for 15 to 20 minutes till golden brown.
7. Remove from the oven and eat at once.

Duck with Blackcurrants

1	Medium	Duck Breast, boned and skinned
2	Tablespoons	Blackcurrant Jam
2	Medium	Spring Onions
1	Medium	Carrot
1	Tablespoon	Ground Nut Oil
1	Teaspoon	Soy Sauce

1. Cut duck into thin strips and place in a bowl.
2. Now mix together in a bowl the soy sauce and jam add the meat and stir well.
3. Peel and cut carrot into thin strips.
4. Clean spring onions and chop.
5. Heat a large frying pan or wok and add oil.
6. Add carrots and spring onions and stir fry for 1 minute until golden brown.
7. Now add meat and stir fry for another 3 minutes.

Serving Suggestion
Serve on a bed of rice or noodles.

Duck with Orange

1	Medium	Duck Breast, boned and skinned
1	Medium	Orange
2	Medium	Spring Onions
1	Medium	Carrot
1	Tablespoon	Ground Nut Oil
1	Teaspoon	Soy Sauce
1	Teaspoon	Cornflour

1. Cut duck into thin strips and place in a bowl.
2. Grate rind from orange and remove the juice.
3. Add to duck mix well and let marinate in the refrigerator.
4. After at least 20 minutes drain liquid from meat and keep to one side.
5. Now mix together in a bowl the soy sauce and sesame oil add the meat.
6. Peel and cut carrot into thin strips.
7. Clean spring onions and chop.
8. Heat a large frying pan or wok and add oil.
9. Add meat and stir-fry for 1 minute until golden brown.
10. Now add carrots and spring onions and stir-fry for another 3 minutes.
11. Mix the orange marinate with the cornflour and pour into pan stirring until boiling and thicken.

Serving Suggestion
Serve on a bed of rice or noodles.

Edam Stuffed Brown Pasta Quills

12	Large	Brown Pasta Quills
½	Cup	Edam Cheese
½	Cup	Finely Diced Red Pepper
1	Tablespoon	Chopped Walnuts
1	Tablespoon	Chopped Black Olives
1	Teaspoon	Chopped Parsley
1	Teaspoon	Dried Oregano

1. Place the pasta in a pot of boiling sated water; cook the pasta quills as directed on package or until they are al dente (firm but cooked).
2. Rinse the cooked pasta under cold running water and drain well.
3. Arrange the pasta on plate and set aside.
4. In medium bowl, mix the cheese, red pepper, olives, walnuts, parsley and oregano.
5. Fill each pasta quill with about 1 teaspoon of the cheese mixture.
6. Place plate under a grill until the cheese melts.
7. Serve at once.

Gammon Steak with Pineapple Sauce

1	Medium	Gammon Steak
1	Teaspoon	Honey
1	Teaspoon	Dijon Mustard
½	Cup	Tin Pineapple Bits

1. Trim the gammon steak and wipe with kitchen paper.
2. Grill under a medium heat for 4 minutes on each side.
3. In a bowl mix the honey, mustard and pineapple bits.
4. Spread mix on top of the steak grill for 8 minutes until crispy.

Goujons Chicken

1	Large	Chicken Breast
1	Cup	Breadcrumbs, fresh
1	Teaspoon	Ground Coriander
1	Teaspoon	Ground Cumin
1	Teaspoon	Ground Paprika
1	Pinch	Salt & Pepper
2	Tablespoons	Flour
1	Medium	Egg

1. Remove any skin from chicken and wipe with kitchen paper.
2. Place breast between two sheets of cling film and pound flat.
3. Cut the chicken into thin strips, then place the flour in a bowl and toss the chicken in it.
4. In a bowl mix together the breadcrumbs, herbs and seasoning.
5. Beat the egg in a bowl and then dip the floured chicken in it then coat with the breadcrumb mixture.
6. Cook in deep oil until the chicken is golden brown

Serving Suggestion
Serve with the garlic dip or cucumber dip

Goujons Turkey

1	Large	Turkey Breast
1	Cup	Breadcrumbs, fresh
1	Teaspoon	Ground Coriander
1	Teaspoon	Ground Cumin
1	Teaspoon	Ground Paprika
1	Pinch	Salt & Pepper
2	Tablespoons	Flour
1	Medium	Egg

1. Remove any skin from turkey and wipe with kitchen paper.
2. Place breast between two sheets of cling film and pound flat.
3. Cut the turkey into thin strips, then place the flour in a bowl and toss the turkey in it.
4. In a bowl mix together the breadcrumbs, herbs and seasoning.
5. Beat the egg in a bowl and then dip the floured turkey in it then coat with the breadcrumb mixture.
6. Cook in deep oil until the turkey is golden brown

Serving Suggestion
Serve with the garlic dip or cucumber dip

Grilled Cod with a Whisky Sauce

1	Thick	Cod Steak
1	Medium	Egg Yolk
2	Tablespoons	Butter
1	Cup	Hot Water
½	Whole	Fish Stock Cube
1	Tablespoon	Scotch Whisky
1	Tablespoon	Double Cream
1	Pinch	Cayenne Pepper

1. Place the fish in an ovenproof dish under a moderate heated grill.
2. Dot the fish with 1 tablespoon of the butter and place under the grill, turn fish once during cooking.
3. Grill until firm and lightly golden on top, about 4 minutes.
4. Place a saucepan over a medium heat add the other tablespoon of butter let melt.
5. Mix stock cube with water and add to pan also add the cream, egg yolk and whisky, stir well cook for 4 to 5 minutes to thicken.
6. To serve place fish on a warm plate and pour sauce over and sprinkle the cayenne pepper over it.

Grilled Lamb Chop with Mustard

2	Medium	Lamb Chops
1	Tablespoon	Extra Virgin Olive Oil
1	Pinch	Salt & Pepper
2	Tablespoons	Dijon Mustard

1. Trim the chops and wipe with kitchen paper.
2. Brush with the extra virgin olive oil dust with a little salt and pepper then spread the mustard on both sides.
3. Cook under a hot grill for 6-7 minutes each side turning frequently.

Serving Suggestion
To serve place on a warm plate and add cooked vegetables.

Grilled Salmon with a Schnapps Sauce

1	Thick	Salmon Steak
1	Medium	Egg Yolk
2	Tablespoons	Butter
1	Cup	Hot Water
½	Whole	Fish Stock Cube
1	Tablespoon	Schnapps
1	Tablespoon	Double Cream
1	Pinch	Cayenne Pepper

1. Place the fish in an ovenproof dish under a moderate heated grill.
2. Dot the fish with 1 tablespoon of the butter and place under the grill, turn fish once during cooking.
3. Grill until firm and lightly golden on top, about 4 minutes.
4. Place a saucepan over a medium heat add the other tablespoon of butter let melt.
5. Mix stock cube with water and add to pan also add the cream, egg yolk and schnapps, stir well cook for 4 to 5 minutes to thicken.
6. To serve place fish on a warm plate and pour sauce over and sprinkle the cayenne pepper over it.

Halibut with Cheese Sauce

1	Fillet	Halibut
2	Cups	Milk
2	Cloves	Garlic, chopped
2	Tablespoons	Strong Cooking Cheese, grated
2	Tablespoons	Mozzarella Cheese, grated
1	Teaspoon	Italian Seasoning
1	Tablespoon	Butter
1	Tablespoon	Cornflour
1	Pinch	Salt & Pepper

1. Place a saucepan over a medium heat add the butter and melt then add the cornflour and cook for 1 to 2 minutes stiring all the time.
2. Slowly add the milk, salt, pepper, garlic, Italian seasoning and cooking cheese stir well and increase the heat and cook for 4 minutes until sauce thickens.
3. Place the fish into an ovenproof dish pour over the sauce and sprinkle with the mozzarella cheese.
4. Bake in a moderate oven at 375°F, 190°C or Gas Mark 5 for 18 to 20 minutes till golden brown.

Italian Lamb Crumble

2	Cups	Lean Minced Lamb
1	Small Tin	Tomatoes, chopped
1	Small	Onion, finely chopped
1	Teaspoon	Tomato Puree
2	Cloves	Garlic, crushed
1	Teaspoon	Italian Seasoning
1	Cup	Plain Flour
½	Cup	Butter
2	Tablespoons	Cheese, grated

1. Heat a frying pan over a moderate heat add lamb, onions and garlic, stir until meat browns and separates into grains.
2. Add chopped tomatoes, tomato puree and Italian seasoning.
3. Bring to the boil then reduce heat stir from time to time.
4. Cook for about 14 to 18 minutes until sauce thickens.
5. In a bowl rub the butter into the flour until it looks like breadcrumbs then add cheese and mix well.
6. Place sauce into an ovenproof dish and cover with the crumble mix.
7. Bake in a moderate oven at 350°F, 180°C or Gas Mark 4 for 20 to 25 minutes.

Lamb Hotpot

1	Medium	Lamb Chop
2	Whole	Potatoes, very thinly sliced
1	Small	Leek, sliced
1	Small	Onion, finely chopped
1	Whole	Carrot, sliced
1	Clove	Garlic, grated
1	Tablespoon	Butter
1		Lamb Stock Cube
2	Cups	Warm Water
1	Pinch	Salt & Pepper
1	Teaspoon	Mixed Herbs

1. Trim the chop and wipe with kitchen paper.
2. Place chop in an ovenproof casserole dish.
3. Add onions, leeks, and carrots.
4. Now sprinkle with the herbs, salt and pepper.
5. Arrange the sliced potatoes evenly over the top of chop.
6. Mix lamb stock in water and pour over potatoes.
7. Brush the potatoes with the butter and cover with a lid or tin foil.
8. Bake in a moderate oven at 350°F, 180 °C or Gas Mark 4 for about 60 minutes.
9. Then remove the cover and cook for about 10 minute until top is golden brown.
10. Serve at once on a warm plate.

Plaice with Cheese Sauce

1	Fillet	Plaice
2	Cups	Milk
2	Cloves	Garlic, chopped
2	Tablespoons	Strong Cooking Cheese, grated
2	Tablespoons	Mozzarella Cheese, grated
1	Teaspoon	Italian seasoning
1	Tablespoon	Butter
1	Tablespoon	Cornflour
1	Pinch	Salt & Pepper

1. Place a saucepan over a medium heat add the butter and melt then add the cornflour and cook for 1 to 2 minutes stirring all the time.
2. Slowly add the milk, salt, pepper, garlic, Italian seasoning and cooking cheese stir well and increase the heat and cook for 4 minutes until sauce thickens.
3. Place the fish into an ovenproof dish pour over the sauce and sprinkle with the mozzarella cheese.
4. Bake in a moderate oven at 375°F, 190°C or Gas Mark 5 for 18 to 20 minutes till golden brown.

Prawn Chop Suey

1	Tablespoon	Nut Oil
1	Small	Finely Chopped Onion,
1	Small	Finely Chopped Red Pepper
1	Small	Finely Chopped Yellow Pepper
1	Large	Finely Grated Carrot
1	Stick	Finely Chopped Celery
1	Small	Tin Bean Sprouts
2	Cups	Sliced Cooked Prawn
1	Teaspoon	Light Soy Sauce
¼		Vegetable Stock Cube
2	Tablespoons	Water

1. Heat a wok or a deep frying pan over a moderate heat add the oil
2. Now add the onion, red pepper, yellow pepper, carrot and celery and stir-fry for 1 to 2 minutes.
3. Add the bean sprouts and prawn stir well then add the stock cube, water and soy sauce stir-fry for another 1 to 2 minutes until cooked.

Serving Suggestion
Serve on a bed of rice

Sauté Prawns

1	Tablespoons	Butter.
2	Cloves	Garlic, crushed.
1	Cup	Prawns, cooked.
1	Slice	White Bread.

1. Place a frying pan over a moderate heat, add the butter and melt it.
2. Add the crushed garlic to the frying pan and sauté for 3 to 4 minutes.
3. Remove the crusts from the slice of white bread and roll it flat with a rolling pin.
4. Toast both sides of the cut bread, until it is a light golden colour.
5. Add the prawns to the frying pan and stirring well for 1 to 2 minutes just to warm the prawns through.
6. Place the toasted bread on a warm plate and top with the prawns and garlic mixture.

Steak & Mushroom Pie

1	Portion	Beef Fillet Steak
½	Pack	Frozen Puff Pastry Shell
1	Cup	Button Mushrooms
1	Whole	Beef Stock Cube
1	Small	Onion thinly sliced
2	Tablespoons	Butter
1	Pinch	Salt & Pepper
2	Cups	Water

1. Cut steak into thin strips about an inch long.
2. Heat a fry pan and add 1 tablespoon of the butter.
3. Add onions and sauté for 2 to 3 minutes until softened.
4. Now add mushrooms to pan and sauté them both for a further 2 minutes.
5. Add beef and sauté for about 3 to 5 minutes then add salt and pepper.
6. Mix water with stock cube and add to pan.
7. Cook for about 5 minutes until the sauce thickens.
8. Roll out the pastry and line a small pie dish.
9. Fill dish with beef mix then cover with pastry.
10. Brush top of pie with butter and make a small slit in it.
11. Bake in a moderate oven at 400°F, 200°C or Gas Mark 5 for 15 to 20 minutes until well raised and golden brown.

Steak with Mushrooms & Schnapps

1	Portion	Beef Fillet Steak
1	Cup	Button Mushrooms
1	Small	Onion, thinly sliced
2	Tablespoons	Butter
1	Tablespoon	Schnapps
¼	Cup	Cream
1	Pinch	Salt & Pepper

1. Cut steak into thin strips about an inch long.
2. Heat a fry pan and add 1 tablespoon of the butter.
3. Add onions and sauté for 2 to 3 minutes until softened.
4. Now add mushrooms to pan and sauté them both for a further 2 minutes.
5. Remove from pan and add remaining butter to pan and melt.
6. Add beef and sauté for about 3 to 5 minutes.
7. Now add schnapps to beef in pan and ignite shake pan until flames subside.
8. Return mushrooms and onions to pan and stir in cream.
9. Cook for about 1 minute until all the ingredients are well heated.

Serving Suggestion
Serve at once on a warm plate.

Puddings

Almond & Dark Chocolate Mousse	131
Almond & White Chocolate Mousse	132
Apple & Cheddar Cheese Crumble	133
Apple & Stilton Crumble	134
Apricot Sorbet	135
Baked Alaska	136
Baked Apple with Calvados	137
Baked Apple with Whisky	138
Baked Lemon Pudding	139
Baked Orange Pudding	140
Banana Pudding	141
Banana Sorbet	142
Basic Crepes	143
Bread & Butter Pudding	144
Bread & Butter Pudding with Golden Syrup	145
Bread & Butter Pudding with Honey	146
Cherry Cheesecake	147
Chocolate Crepes	148
Chocolate Egg Custard	149
Chocolate Pizza	150
Crepes with Blackcurrants and Ice Cream	151
Crepes with Raspberries & Ice Cream	152
Crepes with Strawberries & Ice Cream	153
Currant Steamed Pudding	154

Egg Custard	155
Fruit Steamed Pudding	156
Lemon Cheesecake	157
Malt Bread & Butter Pudding	158
Mango Cloud	159
Mango Sorbet	160
Mincemeat Parcels	161
Nectarine & Cheese Crumble	162
Orange Egg Custard	163
Pineapple Delight	164
Raisin Steamed Pudding	165
Raspberry Soufflé	166
Spiced Peach Crumble	167
Strawberry Cloud	168
Strawberry Delight	169
Summer Fruits Soufflé	170

Almond & Dark Chocolate Mousse

1	Small	Egg
1	Small Bar	Dark Chocolate
1	Tablespoon	Sugar
2	Tablespoon	Boiling Water
1	Tablespoon	Chopped Blanched Almonds
1	Teaspoon	Almond Extract

1. Break egg and separate the yolk from the white.
2. Place white into a clean medium sized bowl.
3. Now beat egg white until foamy then gradually add the sugar and continue beating until stiff.
4. Place chocolate; egg yolk, boiling water and flavouring into a blender and blend for few seconds until chocolate is melted.
5. Fold chocolate mixture into egg white until no streaks of egg white remain.
6. Turn into a ramekin dish, and chill in a refrigerator for several hours until firm.
7. Remove from the refrigerator and serve at once.

Almond & White Chocolate Mousse

1	Small	Egg
1	Small Bar	White Chocolate
1	Tablespoon	Sugar
2	Tablespoon	Boiling Water
1	Tablespoon	Chopped Blanched Almonds
1	Teaspoon	Almond Extract

1. Break egg and separate the yolk from the white.
2. Place egg white into a clean medium sized bowl.
3. Now beat egg white until foamy then gradually add the sugar and continue beating until stiff.
4. Place chocolate; egg yolk, boiling water and flavouring into a blender and blend for few seconds until chocolate is melted.
5. Fold chocolate mixture into egg white until no streaks of egg white remain.
6. Turn into a ramekin dish, and chill in a refrigerator for several hours until firm.
7. Remove from the refrigerator and serve at once.

Apple & Cheddar Cheese Crumble

1	Large	Cooking Apple
1	Teaspoon	Ground Cinnamon
2	Teaspoons	Brown Sugar
¼	Cup	Grated Cheddar Cheese
1	Tablespoon	SR Flour
1	Tablespoon	Rolled Oats
1	Tablespoon	Butter

1. Preheat oven to 375°F, 190°C or Gas Mark 5.
2. Grease a large ramekin dish.
3. Peel and core the apple and cut into pieces.
4. Mix together the apple, cinnamon, and 1 teaspoon of the brown sugar.
5. Place in the botton of a large ramekin dish.
6. In a small bowl, mix cheese, flour, oats and the other teaspoon of sugar then add butter.
7. Combine the mixture together with your fingers until it resembles breadcrumbs.
8. Cover apple with the crumble mixture.
9. Bake until apple is tender and topping is light brown about 25 to 30 minutes.
10. Remove from oven and serve at once.

Serving Suggestion
To serve pour over a little custard or drizzle with fresh cream.

Apple & Stilton Crumble

1	Large	Cooking Apple
1	Teaspoon	Ground Cinnamon
2	Teaspoons	Brown Sugar
¼	Cup	Grated Stilton Cheese
1	Tablespoon	SR Flour
1	Tablespoon	Rolled Oats
1	Tablespoon	Butter

1. Preheat oven to 375°F, 190°C or Gas Mark 5.
2. Grease a large ramekin dish.
3. Peel and core the apple and cut into pieces.
4. Mix together the apple, cinnamon, and 1 teaspoon of the brown sugar..
5. Place in the botton of a large ramekin dish.
6. In a small bowl, mix cheese, flour, oats and the other teaspoon of sugar then add butter.
7. Combine the mixture together with your fingers until it resembles breadcrumbs.
8. Cover apple with the crumble mixture.
9. Bake until apple is tender and topping is light brown about 25 to 30 minutes.
10. Remove from oven and serve at once.

Serving Suggestion
To serve pour over a little custard or drizzle with fresh cream.

Apricot Sorbet

6	Medium	Apricots
1	Tablespoon	White Wine
1	Teaspoon	Lime Juice
1	Medium	Egg White

1. Peel the apricots and cut off the flesh from around the stone.
2. Put flesh into a blender or food processor and blend until it's a smooth purée.
3. Into a mixing bowl put the wine and limejuice and add the purée and mix well.
4. Place purée in a freezer container and freeze until it is just beginning to set around the edges.
5. Remove from freezer and break up the ice crystals.
6. Then whisk the egg white until it is stiff and fold into purée mixture.
7. Return to freezer until completely set.
8. Remove from the freezer to serve just spoon the required amount into serving dish.

Baked Alaska

¼	Cup	White SR Flour
1	Small	Egg
2	Tablespoons	Butter
¼	Teaspoon	Cream of Tartar
1	Teaspoon	Water
3	Drops	Vanilla Extract
2	Tablespoon	Sugar
1	Tablespoon	Strawberry Jam
1	Portion	Strawberry Ice Cream

1. Cream the butter and sugar together in a medium bowl until very pale in colour, add flour, egg yolk, water and vanilla extract, beat again until smooth and creamy.
2. Grease a small cake tin and line the bottom and sides with greaseproof paper.
3. Pour the sponge mixture into prepared tin and cook in a moderate oven at 350°F, 180°C or Gas Mark 4, for 8 to 10 minutes or until golden brown and firm to the touch.
4. Remove from the oven and turn on to a wire rack to cool, after a few minutes remove the paper.
5. For the meringue, put the egg white in to a clean dry bowl and add cream of tartar, beat well then gradually add sugar, beating until stiff peaks form.
6. Place cake, bottom side up, on an ovenproof platter and spread with the strawberry jam, add the portion of strawberry ice cream, spread the meringue over ice cream and around the sides of cake.
7. Bake in a hot oven at 450°F, 230°C or Gas Mark 8 for 2 minutes until golden brown.
8. Remove from the oven and serve at once.

Baked Apple with Calvados

¼	Cup	Glacé Cherries
1	Tablespoon	Brown Sugar
½	Teaspoon	Ground Cinnamon
¼	Teaspoon	Lemon Rind, grated
1	Tablespoon	Calvados
1	Large	Cooking Apple
1	Teaspoon	Clear Honey
2	Cups	Hot Water

1. Combine glacé cherries, brown sugar, cinnamon, lemon rind, and calvados in a small bowl.
2. Core apple three quarters of the way through being careful not to cut through the bottom.
3. Place the apple in a small dish.
4. Fill centre of apples with the mixture and drizzle the honey over top of apple.
5. Set the dish into a baking tin now add enough boiling water into baking tin to come half way up the sides of the dish.
6. During cooking keep basting the apple with syrup from dish and top up the water if needed.
7. Bake in a preheated oven at 400°F, 200°C or Gas Mark 6 for 40 minutes or until tender.
8. Remove from the oven and serve at once.

Serving Suggestion
To serve pour over syrup or try serving with little custard or drizzle with fresh cream.

Baked Apple with Whisky

¼	Cup	Glacé Cherries
1	Tablespoon	Brown Sugar
½	Teaspoon	Ground Cinnamon
¼	Teaspoon	Lemon Rind, grated
1	Tablespoon	Whisky
1	Large	Cooking Apple
1	Teaspoon	Clear Honey
2	Cups	Hot Water

1. Combine glacé cherries, brown sugar, cinnamon, lemon rind, and whisky in a small bowl.
2. Core apple three quarters of the way through being careful not to cut through the bottom.
3. Place the apple in a small dish.
4. Fill centre of apples with the mixture and drizzle the honey over top of apple.
5. Set the dish into a baking tin now add enough boiling water into baking tin to come half way up the sides of the dish.
6. During cooking keep basting the apple with syrup from dish and top up the water if needed.
7. Bake in a preheated oven at 400°F, 200°C or Gas Mark 6 for 40 minutes or until tender.
8. Remove from the oven and serve at once.

Serving Suggestion
To serve pour over syrup or try serving with little custard or drizzle with fresh cream.

Baked Lemon Pudding

2	Tablespoons	Soft Butter
?	Cup	Sugar
¼	Cup	White SR Flour
1	Medium	Egg Yolk
1	Tablespoon	Lemon Juice
1	Teaspoon	Grated Lemon Rind

1. Cream the butter and sugar together in a medium bowl until very pale in colour.
2. Add flour, egg yolk, lemon rind, lemon juice, and beat again until smooth and creamy.
3. Grease tin and line with bottom and side with greaseproof paper.
4. Pour Sponge mixture into prepared tin and cook in a moderate oven at 350°F, 180°C or Gas Mark 4.
5. For 8 to 10 minutes or until golden brown and firm to the touch.
6. Remove from the oven and serve warm with a little custard or drizzle with fresh cream.

Baked Orange Pudding

2	Tablespoons	Soft Butter
?	Cup	Sugar
¼	Cup	White SR Flour
1	Medium	Egg Yolk
1	Tablespoon	Orange Juice
1	Teaspoon	Grated Orange Rind

1. Cream the butter and sugar together in a medium bowl until very pale in colour.
2. Add flour, egg yolk, orange rind, orange juice, and beat again until smooth and creamy.
3. Grease tin and line the bottom and side with greaseproof paper.
4. Pour sponge mixture into prepared tin and cook in a moderate oven at 350°F, 180°C or Gas Mark 4, for 8 to 10 minutes or until golden brown and firm to the touch.
5. Remove from the oven and serve warm with a little custard or drizzle with fresh cream.

Banana Pudding

½	Cup	Milk
1	Small	Egg Yolk
1	Teaspoon	Cornflour
1	Pinch	Salt
1	Sliced	Ripe Banana
3	Drops	Vanilla Extract
4	Small	Vanilla Wafers

1. Place the milk, egg yolk, cornflour and the vanilla extract in a saucepan and stir well.
2. Place over medium heat and simmer for about 7 minutes or until smooth and thickened, stirring constantly.
3. Remove from heat; stir in banana and mix well.
4. Arrange the 4 wafers around the side of a small dish then pour in the mixture.
5. Cover with cling film chill in a refrigerator for at least 2 hours.
6. To serve remove from refrigerator turn upside on a plate and remove dish.

Banana Sorbet

2	Medium	Bananas
1	Teaspoon	Lime Juice
1	Medium	Egg White
1	Tablespoon	White Wine

1. Peel the banana and cut into slices.
2. Put slices into a blender or food processor and blend unto a smooth purée.
3. Into a mixing bowl put the wine and limejuice, add the purée and mix well.
4. Place purée mixture in a freezer container and freeze until it just beginning to set around the edges.
5. Remove from freezer and break up the ice crystals.
6. Then whisk the egg white until it is stiff and fold into purée mixture.
7. Return to freezer until completely set.
8. To serve just spoon required amount into a serving dish.

Basic Crepes

1½	Cups	SR Flour White
1	Cup	Milk
½	Cup	Water
1	Tablespoon	Sugar
1	Large	Egg

1. Add all the ingredients to a mixing bowl and blend on high speed for 1 minute with an electric mixer or for 5 minutes with a hand balloon whisk.
2. Refrigerate mixture for 2 hours or over night.
3. Place a 6" frying pan or omelette pan over a medium heat brush the bottom and sides of pan with the vegetable oil.
4. Then pour in ¼ cup of the batter into the pan; tipping pan to coat bottom with batter then using spatula gently pull it away from end of pan.
5. Cook until top is just set and bottom is lightly browned then with a spatula, turn the crepe over and cook the other side for about 1 minute.
6. Repeat the procedure until all batter is used.

Bread & Butter Pudding

3	Slices	White Bread
1	Cup	Evaporated Milk
1	Medium	Egg
1	Tablespoon	Butter
¼	Cup	Raisins
1	Tablespoon	Mixed Dried Fruit
1	Tablespoon	Sugar

1. Spread the bread with the butter.
2. Cut into quarters and place in a small ovenproof dish.
3. Sprinkle the mixed dried fruit over the bread.
4. Mix together the milk, egg, and sugar.
5. Pour over bread and let soak for a few minutes.
6. Bake in a moderate oven at 350°F, 180°C or Gas Mark 4 for about 35 to 40 minutes.
7. Serve at once.

Bread & Butter Pudding with Golden Syrup

3	Slices	White Bread
1	Cup	Evaporated milk
1		Egg
1	Tablespoon	Butter
1	Tablespoon	Golden Syrup
1	Tablespoon	Sugar

1. Spread the bread with the butter and the syrup.
2. Cut into quarters and place in a small ovenproof dish.
3. Mix together the milk, egg, and sugar.
4. Pour over bread and let soak for a few minutes.
5. Bake in a moderate oven at 350°F, 180°C or Gas Mark 4 for about 35 to 40 minutes.
6. Remove from the oven and serve at once.

Bread & Butter Pudding with Honey

3	Slices	White Bread
1	Cup	Evaporated milk
1		Egg
1	Tablespoon	Butter
1	Tablespoon	Honey
1	Tablespoon	Sugar

1. Spread the bread with the butter and the honey.
2. Cut into quarters and place in a small ovenproof dish.
3. Mix together the milk, egg, and sugar.
4. Pour over bread and let soak for a few minutes.
5. Bake in a moderate oven at 350°F, 180°C or Gas Mark 4 for about 35 to 40 minutes.
6. Remove from the oven and serve at once.

Cherry Cheesecake

½	Cup	Cottage Cheese
¼	Small Can	Cherry Pie Filling
¼	Cup	Double Cream
1	Teaspoon	Sugar
1	Teaspoon	Lemon Juice
2	Teaspoons	Soft Butter
3	Whole	Digestive Biscuits

1. In a bowl crush the digestive biscuits and add the soft butter and mix well.
2. Cover a small plate with a sheet of cling and place a muffin ring on it.
3. Fill with the biscuit mix to cover the base push down hard with the back of a spoon.
4. Rub the cheese through a sieve into a bowl and add lemon juice mix well.
5. Whip the cream until thick and fold into the cheese mix.
6. Put cheese mix into muffin ring, level with top, spread the pie filling on top and chill for an hour.
7. To serve place on a plate and remove the muffin ring and cling film.

Chocolate Crepes

1½	Cups	White SR Flour
1	Cup	Milk
½	Cup	Water
2	Tablespoons	Vegetable Oil
1	Tablespoon	Cocoa Powder
1	Tablespoon	Sugar
1	Large	Egg

1. Add all the ingredients to a mixing bowl and blend on high speed for 1 minute with an electric mixer or for 5 minutes with a hand balloon whisk.
2. Refrigerate mixture for 2 hours or overnight.
3. Place a 6" frying pan or omelette pan over a medium heat, brush the bottom and sides of pan with the vegetable oil.
4. Then pour in ¼ cup of the batter into the pan; tipping pan to coat bottom with batter then using spatula gently pull it away from edge of pan.
5. Cook until top is just set and bottom is lightly browned, then with a spatula, turn the crepe over and cook the other side for about 1 minute.
6. Repeat the procedure until all batter is used.

Chocolate Egg Custard

1	Cup	Milk
1	Medium	Egg, beaten
2	Tablespoons	Milk Chocolate
1	Tablespoon	Sugar
1	Teaspoon	Vanilla

1. Warm the milk in a saucepan and add the chocolate and melt.
2. Break the egg into bowl and add the vanilla and sugar then whisk together.
3. Pour hot milk into the egg mixture whisking all the time.
4. Pour the custard mixture into a ramekin dish and set the ramekin dish into a deep baking tin.
5. Now add enough boiling water into baking tray to come half way up the sides of the ramekin dish.
6. Bake in a moderate oven at 325°F, 160°C or Gas Mark 3, for 20 to 25 minutes.

Chocolate Pizza

1	Cup	SR Flour
2	Tablespoons	Butter
1	Tablespoon	Water
1	Teaspoon	Salt
1	Teaspoon	Cocoa Powder
½	Cup	Chocolate Chips
2	Tablespoons	Walnuts, chopped

1. In a bowl mix the flour, sugar, cocoa powder, water and butter to a stiff dough.
2. Roll out the dough on a floured surface into a circle.
3. Then place onto a greased baking sheet.
4. Bake in a moderate oven at 400°F, 200°C or Gas Mark 6 for 10 to 12 minutes till golden brown.
5. Remove from the oven and sprinkle the chocolate chips over it and top with the chopped walnuts

Crepes with Blackcurrants and Ice Cream

1½	Cups	White SR Flour
1	Cup	Milk
½	Cup	Water
1	Tablespoon	Sugar
2	Tablespoons	Vegetable Oil
1	Large	Egg
1	Small Tin	Blackcurrants in Syrup
1	Tablespoon	Cream Sherry
1	Scoop	Vanilla Ice Cream

1. Add the flour, milk, water, egg and sugar to a mixing bowl and mix for 5 minutes with a hand balloon whisk then refrigerate mixture for 2 hours or overnight.
2. Place an omelette pan over a medium heat brush the bottom and sides of pan with the vegetable oil.
3. Then pour in ¼ cup of the batter into the pan; tipping pan to coat bottom with batter then using spatula gently pull it away from edge of pan.
4. Cook until top is just set and bottom is lightly browned then with a spatula, turn the crepe over and cook the other side for about 1 minute, repeat the procedure until all batter is used.
5. Place a pan over a moderate heat, add the blackcurrants and bring to a boil and boil rapidly for a few minutes to reduce the mixture.
6. Reduce the heat, add the sherry and cook for 1 minute.
7. To serve fill each crepe with a small scoop of vanilla ice cream and 3 tablespoons of the sauce.
8. Fold the crepe; pour remaining sauce over the top.

Crepes with Raspberries & Ice Cream

1½	Cups	White SR Flour
1	Cup	Milk
½	Cup	Water
1	Tablespoon	Sugar
2	Tablespoons	Vegetable Oil
1	Large	Egg
1	Small Tin	Raspberries in Syrup
1	Tablespoon	Cream Sherry
1	Scoop	Raspberry Ice Cream

1. Add the flour, milk, water, egg and sugar to a mixing bowl and mix for 5 minutes with a hand balloon whisk then refrigerate mixture for 2 hours or overnight.
2. Place an omelette pan over a medium heat brush the bottom and sides of pan with the vegetable oil.
3. Then pour in ¼ cup of the batter into the pan; tipping pan to coat bottom with batter then using spatula gently pull it away from edge of pan.
4. Cook until top is just set and bottom is lightly browned then with a spatula, turn the crepe over and cook the other side for about 1 minute, repeat the procedure until all batter is used.
5. Place a pan over a moderate heat, add the raspberries and bring to a boil and boil rapidly for a few minutes to reduce the mixture.
6. Reduce the heat, add the sherry and cook for 1 minute.
7. To serve fill each crepe with a small scoop of raspberry ice cream and 3 tablespoons of the sauce.
8. Fold the crepe; pour remaining sauce over the top.

Crepes with Strawberries & Ice Cream

1½	Cups	White SR Flour
1	Cup	Milk
½	Cup	Water
1	Tablespoon	Sugar
1	Large	Egg
2	Tablespoons	Vegetable Oil
1	Small Tin	Strawberries in Syrup
1	Tablespoon	Cream Sherry
1	Scoop	Strawberry Ice Cream

1. Add the flour, milk, water, egg and sugar to a mixing bowl and mix for 5 minutes with a hand balloon whisk then refrigerate mixture for 2 hours or overnight.
2. Place an omelette pan over a medium heat brush the bottom and sides of pan with the vegetable oil.
3. Then pour in ¼ cup of the batter into the pan; tipping pan to coat bottom with batter then using spatula gently pull it away from edge of pan.
4. Cook until top is just set and bottom is lightly browned then with a spatula, turn the crepe over and cook the other side for about 1 minute, repeat the procedure until all batter is used.
5. Place a pan over a moderate heat, add the strawberries and bring to a boil and boil rapidly for a few minutes to reduce the mixture.
6. Reduce the heat, add the sherry and cook for 1 minute.
7. To serve fill each crepe with a small scoop of strawberry ice cream and 3 tablespoons of the sauce.
8. Fold the crepe, pour remaining sauce over the top.

Currant Steamed Pudding

?	Cup	White SR Flour
¼	Cup	Caster Sugar
2	Tablespoons	Butter
2	Tablespoons	Milk
1	Medium	Egg
1	Tablespoon	Currants
1	Pinch	Salt

1. Sift flour and salt into a bowl.
2. Cream butter and sugar until light and fluffy.
3. Beat in the egg, milk and add fruit.
4. Then add the flour a little at a time.
5. Butter a small pudding basin.
6. Put mixture into a basin and cover securely with tin foil.
7. Place in a steamer for 15 to 20 minutes or until firm.
8. Turn out on to a plate and serve.

Egg Custard

1	Cup	Milk
1	Medium	Egg, beaten
1	Teaspoon	Vanilla
1	Tablespoon	Sugar
1	Pinch	Nutmeg

1. Warm the milk in a saucepan.
2. Break the egg into bowl add the vanilla and sugar then whisk together.
3. Pour hot milk into the egg mixture whisking all the time.
4. Pour the custard mixture into a ramekin dish sprinkle with nutmeg.
5. Set the ramekin dish into a deep baking tin.
6. Now add enough boiling water into baking tin to come half way up the sides of the ramekin dish.
7. Bake in a moderate oven at 325°F, 160°C or Gas Mark 3, for 20 to 25 minutes.
8. Remove from the oven and eat at once.

Fruit Steamed Pudding

?	Cup	SR Flour
¼	Cup	Caster Sugar
2	Tablespoons	Butter
2	Tablespoons	Milk
1	Medium	Egg
1	Tablespoon	Fruit, Sultanas, Currants or Raisins
1	Pinch	Salt

1. Sift flour and salt into a bowl.
2. Cream butter and sugar until light and fluffy.
3. Beat in the egg, milk and add fruit.
4. Then the flour a little at a time.
5. Butter a small pudding basin.
6. Put mix into basin and cover securely with tin foil.
7. Place in a steamer for 15 to 20 minutes or until firm.
8. Turn out on to a plate and serve.

Lemon Cheesecake

½	Cup	Cottage Cheese
¼	Cup	Double Cream
1	Teaspoon	Sugar
1	Teaspoon	Lemon Juice
2	Teaspoons	Soft Butter
3	Whole	Digestive Biscuits

1. In a bowl crush the digestive biscuits and add the soft butter and mix well.
2. Cover a small plate with a sheet of cling film place a muffin ring on it.
3. Fill with the biscuit mix to cover the base push down hard with the back of a spoon.
4. Rub the cheese through a sieve into a bowl and add lemon juice mix well.
5. Whip the cream until thick and fold into the cheese mix.
6. Put cheese mix into muffin ring, level with top and chill for an hour.
7. To serve place on a plate and remove the muffin ring and cling film.

Malt Bread & Butter Pudding

3	Slices	Malted Sultana Bread
1	Cup	Evaporated Milk
1	Medium	Egg
1	Tablespoon	Butter
¼	Cup	Raisins
1	Tablespoon	Sugar

1. Spread the bread with the butter.
2. Cut into quarters and place in a small ovenproof dish.
3. Mix together the milk, egg, and sugar.
4. Pour over bread and let soak for a few minutes.
5. Bake in a moderate oven at 350°F, 180°C or Gas Mark 4 for about 35 to 40 minutes.
6. Serve at once.

Mango Cloud

½	Small Tin	Mangos in Syrup
1	Medium	Egg White
½	Cup	Natural Yoghurt

1. Press the fruit through a sieve into a bowl.
2. Discard the pulp and seeds in the sieve.
3. Pour yoghurt into bowl on top of purée and mix well.
4. Now whisk the egg white until it is stiff and fold into the mixture.
5. Spoon the mixture into a ramekin dish and chill.

Mango Sorbet

1	Medium	Mango
1	Teaspoon	Lime Juice
1	Medium	Egg White
1	Tablespoon	White Wine

1. Peel the mango and cut off the flesh from around the stone.
2. Put flesh into a blender or food processor and blend until it's a smooth purée.
3. Into a mixing bowl put the wine and limejuice and add the purée and mix well.
4. Place purée in a freezer container and freeze until it just beginning to set around the edges.
5. Remove from freezer and break up the ice crystals.
6. Then whisk the egg white until it is stiff and fold into purée mixture.
7. Return to freezer until completely set.
8. To serve just spoon into serving dish.

Mincemeat Parcels

4	Tablespoons	Mincemeat
2	Sheets	Filo Pastry
2	Tablespoons	Butter
1	Tablespoon	Icing Sugar

1. Lay the sheets of filo pastry flat and brush them with the butter
2. Now fold each in half and place 2 tablespoons of mincemeat in the middle each of the sheets
3. Now draw up all the sides and squeeze the top together brush with the butter.
4. Transfer to a buttered baking sheet
5. Bake in a moderate oven at 375°F, 190°C or Gas Mark 5 for 12 to 18 minutes till golden brown.
6. Remove from the oven and dust with the icing sugar

Nectarine & Cheese Crumble

1	Large	Nectarine
1	Teaspoon	Ground Cinnamon
2	Teaspoons	Brown Sugar
¼	Cup	Grated Cheddar Cheese
1	Tablespoon	SR Flour
1	Tablespoon	Rolled Oats
1	Tablespoon	Butter

1. Preheat oven to 375°F, 190°C or Gas Mark 5.
2. Grease a large ramekin dish.
3. Peel and remove stone from the nectarine and cut into pieces.
4. Mix together the nectarine, cinnamon, and 1 teaspoons of the brown sugar..
5. Place in the botton of a large ramekin dish.
6. In a small bowl, mix cheese, flour, oats and the other teaspoon of sugar then add butter.
7. Combine the mixture together with your fingers until it resembles breadcrumbs.
8. Cover nectarine with the crumble mixture.
9. Bake until nectarine is tender and topping is light brown about 25 to 30 minutes.
10. Remove from oven and serve at once.

Serving Suggestion
To serve pour over a little custard or drizzle with fresh cream.

Orange Egg Custard

1	Cup	Milk
1	Medium	Egg, beaten
1	Tablespoon	Orange Marmalade Fine Cut
1	Tablespoon	Sugar
1	Teaspoon	Vanilla

1. Warm the milk in a saucepan.
2. Break the egg into a bowl add the vanilla, marmalade and sugar then whisk together.
3. Pour hot milk into the egg mixture whisking all the time.
4. Pour the custard mixture into a ramekin dish and set the ramekin dish into a deep baking tin.
5. Now add enough boiling water into baking tin to come half way up the side of the dish.
6. Bake in a moderate oven at 325°F, 160°C or Gas Mark 3 20 to 25 minutes.

Pineapple Delight

1	Cup	Vanilla Yoghurt
½	Cup	Canned Pineapple
5	Whole	Ice Cubes
1	Teaspoon	Wheat germ
3	Drops	Vanilla Extract
2	Cups	Milk

1. Combine all the ingredients in blender container,.
2. Blend until smooth, about 20 seconds.

Serving Suggestion
Pour into a glass and drink at once.

Raisin Steamed Pudding

?	Cup	White SR Flour
¼	Cup	Caster Sugar
2	Tablespoons	Butter
2	Tablespoons	Milk
1	Medium	Egg
1	Tablespoon	Raisins
1	Pinch	Salt

1. Sift flour and salt into a bowl.
2. Cream butter and sugar until light and fluffy.
3. Beat in the egg, milk and add fruit.
4. Then add the flour a little at a time.
5. Butter a small pudding basin.
6. Put mix into basin and cover securely with tin foil.
7. Place in a steamer for 15 to 20 minutes or until firm.
8. Turn out on to a plate and serve.

Raspberry Soufflé

½	Tin	Raspberries in Syrup
1	Teaspoon	Sugar
1	Medium	Egg
1	Tablespoon	Butter
1	Tablespoon	White SR Flour

1. Place a saucepan over a low heat add the butter and melt with a wooden spoon stir in the flour and cook for 2 minutes.
2. Now slowly add the fruit to the saucepan stir with a whisk until the sauce thickens then bring to the boil and simmer for 2 to 3 minutes.
3. Stir in the sugar and let cool.
4. Separate the egg and beat the yolk into the sauce mixture.
5. Then whisk the egg white until it is stiff and fold into sauce mixture.
6. Spoon the mixture into a buttered ramekin dish and bake at 400°F, 200°C or Gas Mark 6 for 15 to 20 minutes until golden brown.

Spiced Peach Crumble

1	Large	Peach
1	Teaspoon	Ground Cinnamon
½	Teaspoon	Allspice
2	Teaspoons	Brown Sugar
1	Tablespoon	SR Flour
1	Tablespoon	Rolled Oats
1	Tablespoon	Butter, cut into small pieces

1. Preheat oven to 375°F, 190°C or Gas Mark 5.
2. Grease a large ramekin dish.
3. Peel, stone and slice the peach.
4. Mix together the peach, ½ teaspoon of cinnamon, and 1 teaspoon of the brown sugar.
5. Place in ramekin dish.
6. In a small bowl, mix the flour, the other ½ teaspoon of cinnamon, allspice, oats, and the other teaspoon of sugar then add butter.
7. Combine the mixture together with your fingers until it resembles breadcrumbs.
8. Cover peaches with the crumble mixture.
9. Bake until peaches are tender and topping is light brown about 25 to 30 minutes.

Serving Suggestion
To serve pour over a little custard or drizzle with fresh cream.

Strawberry Cloud

½	Small Tin	Strawberries in Syrup
1	Medium	Egg White
½	Cup	Natural Yoghurt

1. Press the fruit through a sieve into a bowl.
2. Discard the pulp and seeds in the sieve.
3. Pour yoghurt into bowl on top of purée and mix well.
4. Now whisk the egg white until it is stiff and fold into the mixture.
5. Spoon the mixture into a ramekin dish and chill.

Strawberry Delight

1	Cup	Strawberry Yoghurt
1	Cup	Canned Strawberries
2	Cups	Milk
5	Whole	Ice Cubes
1	Teaspoon	Wheat germ
3	Drops	Vanilla Extract

1. Combine all the ingredients in blender container.
2. Blend until smooth, about 20 seconds.
3. Pour into a glass and drink at once.

Summer Fruits Soufflé

½	Tin	Summer Fruits in Syrup
1	Teaspoon	Sugar
1	Medium	Egg
1	Tablespoon	Butter
1	Tablespoon	SR Flour White

1. Place a saucepan over a low heat add the butter and melt with a wooden spoon stir in the flour and cook for 2 minutes.
2. Now slowly add the fruit to the saucepan stir with a whisk until the sauce thickens then bring to the boil and simmer for 2 to 3 minutes.
3. Stir in the sugar and let cool.
4. Separate the egg and beat the yolk into the sauce mixture.
5. Then whisk the egg white until it is stiff and fold into sauce mixture.
6. Spoon the mixture into a buttered ramekin dish and bake at 400°F, 200°C or Gas Mark 6 for 15 to 20 minutes until golden brown.

Snacks and Suppers

Al-Badinjan	173
Almond Stuffed Dates with Smokey Bacon	174
Apple & Potato Bake	175
Avocado Almonds & Mozzarella Tempura	176
Baked Cajun Fish	177
Baked Onion	178
Beef Burgers Italian	179
Beef Risotto	180
Black Eye Beans Italian	181
Broccoli Lasagne	182
Cajun Al-Badinjan	183
Cajun Black Eye Beans & Rice	184
Carrot & Turnip Soup	185
Celery Soufflé	186
Cheddar Stuffed Brown Pasta Shells	187
Cheese & Mushroom Pizza	188
Cheese & Pineapple Soufflé	189
Chestnuts with Rice	190
Chicken Burgers	191
Christmas Chicken Crackers	192
Crepes with Curried Tuna	193
Crepes with Tuna Garlic and Herbs	194
Deep Dish Pepper & Mushroom Pizza	195
Fish Kebabs	196

Garlic Oven Chips	197
Italian Beef Strudel	198
Italian Tomato Bake	199
Macaroni Cheese	200
Microwave Salmon Steaks	201
Mushroom Soufflé	202
Oven Chips	203
Pork Sausage Toad in the Hole	204
Potato Skins with Cajun Dip	205
Sauté Shrimps & Mushrooms	206
Shrimps on Toast	207
Stuffed Peppers	208
Swiss Eggs	209
Tuna Lasagne with Sweetcorn	210
Tuna Pizza	211
Vegetarian Sausage Toad in the Hole	212

Al-Badinjan

1	Medium	Aubergine
1	Tablespoon	Lime Juice
1	Clove	Garlic, chopped finely
1	Tablespoon	Chopped Fresh Parsley
1	Tablespoon	Olive Oil
1	Teaspoon	Paprika

1. Cook aubergine whole under a hot grill turning as necessary until it is soft throughout and the skin is charred.
2. Set aside to cool then peel the aubergine and discard skin.
3. In a mixing bowl, add the aubergine, limejuice and paprika and mix well.
4. Add salt to taste and the garlic stir well and chill.
5. To serve place on a cold plate dish and garnish with parsley then pour the olive oil over the top

Almond Stuffed Dates with Smokey Bacon

8	Whole	Blanched Almonds
8	Pitted	Dates
8	Rashers	Streak Smokey Bacon

1. Put an almond in each date.
2. Then wrap a rasher of bacon around each stuffed date and secure with a cocktail stick.
3. Line baking sheet with aluminium foil.
4. Then place the dates on the foil and bake in preheated oven at 350°F, 180°C or Gas Mark 4 oven for 12-15 minutes or until bacon is crisp.
5. Remove from the oven and place on a wire rack or paper towel to drain.
6. Serve at once while still warm.

Apple & Potato Bake

1	Tablespoon	Butter
1	Medium	Red Eating Apple
1	Medium	Potato
1	Medium	Onion
1	Tablespoon	Apple Juice
1	Cup	Milk
1	Pinch	Salt & Pepper

1. Peel the apple, potato and cube.
2. Peel the onion and chop finely.
3. Melt the butter in a pan over a medium heat.
4. Add the apple, potato, onion and sauté for 10 minutes.
5. Place into a small ovenproof dish.
6. Add the apple juice, milk, salt and pepper.
7. Bake in a moderate oven at 350°F, 180°C or Gas Mark 4 for 15 to 20 minutes.
8. Remove from the oven and serve at once.

Avocado Almonds & Mozzarella Tempura

2	Small	Chopped Spring Onions
2	Medium	Ripe Avocados, peeled and grated
½	Teaspoon	Ground Coriander
1	Pinch	Salt & Pepper
2	Tablespoons	Lemon Juice
½	Cup	Chopped Almonds
1	Cup	Grated Mozzarella Cheese
½	Cup	White SR Flour
1	Medium	Egg
1	Cup	Fresh White Breadcrumbs

1. Place the chopped onions, grated avocados, salt, pepper, coriander and lemon juice in a bowl and mix with a fork.
2. Stir in the chopped nuts and grated cheese the mixture should be firm.
3. Roll the mixture into walnut sized balls.
4. Place the flour in a bowl and dip the ball in it.
5. Beat the egg in a bowl.
6. Then dip the floured balls in the beaten egg and then dip them in the breadcrumbs.
7. Heat a pan of deep oil and cook the balls until they are golden brown all over.
8. Then remove from the pan and place on kitchen paper to drain.
9. Serve at once while they are still hot.

Baked Cajun Fish

1	Tablespoon	Fresh White Breadcrumbs
1	Tablespoon	Chopped Fresh Parsley
1	Clove	Garlic, crushed
1	Pinch	Salt & Pepper
1	Teaspoon	Cajun Seasoning
1	Teaspoon	Lemon Zest
1	Tablespoon	Extra Virgin Olive Oil
1	Portion	White Fish Fillet

1. In a shallow dish mix together the breadcrumbs, parsley; salt, pepper, Cajun seasoning, lemon zest and crushed garlic.
2. Preheat oven to 325°F, 160°C or Gas Mark 3.
3. Brush the fish fillet on both sides with the olive oil; and then dip into the breadcrumb mixture making sure to coat both sides well.
4. Butter a baking dish and place fish into it and cover with a sheet of tin foil.
5. Bake for 10 to 12 minutes, then remove foil and cook for a further 2 to 3 minutes to let fish brown.
6. Remove fish from the oven and serve at once.

Baked Onion

1	Large	Onion
½	Cup	Fresh White Breadcrumbs
½	Teaspoon	Paprika
½	Teaspoon	Cayenne Pepper
½	Teaspoon	Garlic Powder
1	Small	Beaten Egg
½	Cup	Cottage Cheese
1	Tablespoon	Extra Virgin Olive Oil
1	Tablespoon	Mayonnaise
½	Teaspoon	Horseradish Sauce
1	Pinch	Salt & Pepper

1. Wipe the onion with a damp sheet of kitchen paper then cut 3/4 of the way down as many times as possible.
2. Mix the breadcrumbs, garlic powder, paprika and egg.
3. Spread this over the onion then pour the oil over the onion.
4. Bake in a moderate oven at 375°F, 190°C or Gas Mark 5 for 40-50 minutes.
5. To make the sauce mix the cottage cheese, mayonnaise, horseradish, cayenne, salt and pepper in blender and blend until smooth.
6. Remove the cooked onion from the oven and serve with the sauce

Beef Burgers Italian

2	Cups	Lean Minced Beef
1	Cup	Fresh White Breadcrumbs
1	Small	Finely Chopped Onion
1	Clove	Crushed Garlic
1	Teaspoon	Dried Italian Seasoning
2	Teaspoon	Tomato Puree

1. In a bowl, mix the onion, crushed garlic, beef, breadcrumbs, Italian seasoning and tomato puree.
2. Divide the mixture to make two burgers and pat these in to two round shapes.
3. Grill or fry burgers for 10 to 12 minutes turning once.
4. Serve with tomato relish and salad in burger buns.

Beef Risotto

1	Cup	Diced Cooked Beef
½	Cup	Italian Risotto Rice
2	Cups	Water
1	Small	Chopped Tomato
1	Small	Onion
1	Medium	Yellow Pepper
1	Medium	Green Pepper
1		Beef Stock Cube
1	Tablespoon	Extra Virgin Olive Oil
½	Teaspoon	Salt & Pepper

1. Peel and very finely chop the onion.
2. Chop the peppers and tomato.
3. Heat a saucepan and melt the butter and add the chopped onion, peppers and tomato, sauté for 2 to 3 minutes until they have softened.
4. Now add herbs and rice to pan stir well and cook for another 1 minute.
5. Mix stock cube with water and add to saucepan.
6. Add the stock, tomato, beef, salt and pepper to the pan and bring to the boil.
7. Reduce the heat and simmer for 12 to 15 minutes until all the water has been absorbed and the rice is cooked.
8. To serve pour onto a warm plate and eat at once.

Black Eye Beans Italian

1	Cup	Tined Black Eye Beans
1	Small	Finely Chopped Onion
1	Small Tin	Chopped Tomatoes
1	Tablespoon	Extra Virgin Olive Oil
1	Teaspoon	Tomato Puree
2	Cloves	Garlic
1	Teaspoon	Italian Seasoning
½	Teaspoon	Cinnamon

1. Rinse the black eye beans well.
2. Heat oil in a saucepan and saute onions and garlic for a few minutes.
3. Add the tomatoes and tomato puree.
4. Bring to a boil then lower heat and add the rest of the ingredients.
5. Simmer for about 10 minutes or until the sauce has thickened.

Serving Suggestion
Serve with mashed potatoes and green vegetables or pasta

Broccoli Lasagne

4	Sheets	Lasagne
½	Cup	Creamed Cottage Cheese
2	Cups	Frozen Broccoli
½	Cup	Natural Yoghurt
¼	Cup	Mozzarella Cheese, grated
1	Tablespoon	Yoghurt
1	Pinch	Salt & Pepper

1. Place broccoli into a pan of boiling water and cook for 5 minutes and then drain.
2. Mix cottage cheese natural yoghurt, salt and pepper in a bowl then add the broccoli.
3. In an ovenproof dish place a quarter of the broccoli mix then cover with one sheet of lasagne
4. Repeat this twice.
5. Now add last of mix and sprinkle with the mozzarella cheese.
6. Cover tightly with aluminium foil bake in a moderate oven at 350°F, 180 °C or Gas Mark 4, for 30 minutes or until cheese melts and is golden on top.
7. Remove from the oven and serve on a warm plate, eat at once.

Cajun Al-Badinjan

1	Medium	Aubergine
1	Tablespoon	Lime Juice
1	Clove	Garlic Chopped Finely
1	Tablespoon	Chopped Fresh Parsley
1	Tablespoon	Olive Oil
1	Teaspoon	Cajun Seasoning

1. Cook aubergine whole under a hot grill turning as necessary until it is soft throughout and the skin is charred.
2. Set aside to cool then peel the aubergine and discard skin then place in a mixing bowl.
3. Into the bowl, add the limejuice and cajun seasoning and mix well.
4. Add salt to taste and the garlic stir well and chill.
5. To serve place on a cold plate dish and garnish with parsley then pour the olive oil over the top

Cajun Black Eye Beans & Rice

1	Cup	Tined Black Eye Beans
½	Cup	Chopped Onions
1	Teaspoon	Thyme
1	Teaspoon	Parsley
1	Teaspoon	Blackened Cajun Seasoning
2	Cloves	Garlic, crushed
1	Medium	Yellow Bell Pepper
2	Cups	Cooked Brown Rice
3	Cups	Water
1	Pinch	Salt

1. Rinse beans and drain well.
2. Add the water, beans, cajun seasoning, onion, thyme, garlic, parsley, yellow pepper and salt to a saucepan.
3. Bring to the boil then reduce the heat and simmer over medium heat for 10 to 15 minutes.
4. Then add rice and simmer for another 5 minutes.
5. Serve at once on a warm plate.

Carrot & Turnip Soup

1	Tablespoons	Butter
1	Medium	Peeled & Diced Carrots
1	Medium	Peeled & Diced Turnip
1	Small	Chopped Onion
1	Small	Peeled & Diced Potato
1	Pinch	Salt & Pepper
1	Whole	Vegetable Stock Cube
2	Cups	Warm Water

1. Melt butter in a heavy saucepan over a medium heat.
2. Add the diced carrots, diced turnip, chopped onion and diced potato.
3. Cover and cook over low heat for 5 minutes.
4. Disolve the stock in warm water, then add to pan.
5. Stir and bring to a boil, adding the salt and pepper.
6. Lower the heat and cover, simmer for 25 minutes.
7. Ladle soup into a warm bowl and eat at once.

Serving Suggestion
Serve hot, delicious with home made croûtons.

Celery Soufflé

½	Small Tin	Celery
½	Small Tin	Condensed Celery Soup
1	Large	Egg
1	Pinch	Salt & Pepper

1. Grease a small soufflé dish and empty in the celery.
2. Separate the egg.
3. Empty the celery soup into a bowl and add the egg yolk, salt and pepper and mix together well.
4. Then whisk the egg white until it is stiff fold into egg yolk mixture.
5. Pour over celery and bake at 400°F, 200°C or Gas Mark 6 for 20 to 25 minutes until golden brown.
6. Serve at once on a warm plate.

Serving Suggestion
Try serving with a tomato salad and a whole-wheat roll.

Cheddar Stuffed Brown Pasta Shells

12	Large	Brown Pasta Shells
½	Cup	Cheddar Cheese
½	Cup	Finely Diced Red Pepper
1	Tablespoon	Chopped Walnuts
1	Tablespoon	Chopped Black Olives
1	Teaspoon	Chopped Parsley
1	Teaspoon	Dried Oregano

1. Place the pasta in a pot of boiling sated water; cook the pasta shells as directed on package or until they are al dente (firm but cooked).
2. Rinse the cooked pasta under cold running water and drain well.
3. Arrange the pasta on plate and set aside.
4. In medium bowl, mix the cheese, red pepper, olives, walnuts, parsley and oregano.
5. Fill each pasta shells with about 1 teaspoon of the cheese mixture.
6. Place plate under a grill until the cheese melts.
7. Serve at once.

Cheese & Mushroom Pizza

1	Cup	White SR Flour
2	Tablespoons	Extra Virgin Olive Oil
1	Tablespoon	Water
1	Teaspoon	Salt
1	Small Tin	Tomatoes
1	Teaspoon	Italian Seasoning
1	Cup	Grated Cheese
1	Cup	Chopped Mushrooms

1. In a bowl mix the flour, salt, water and oil to a stiff dough.
2. Roll out the dough on a floured surface into a circle.
3. Then place onto a greased baking sheet.
4. Heat a pan over moderate heat and add tomatoes and herbs bring to the boil and let boil for 5 to 7 minutes until the sauce has reduced by half.
5. Pour over base and top with mushrooms and the cheese.
6. Bake in a moderate oven at 400°F, 200°C or Gas Mark 6 for 15 to 20 minutes till golden brown.
7. Remove from the oven and serve at once.

Cheese & Pineapple Soufflé

½	Cup	Grated Cheese
½	Can	Condensed Chicken Soup
1	Medium	Egg
1	Pinch	Salt & Pepper

1. Greased small soufflé dish.
2. Separate the egg.
3. Empty chicken soup into a bowl, add cheese, egg yolk, salt and pepper and mix together well.
4. Then whisk the egg white until it is stiff fold into yolk mixture.
5. Pour into disk and bake at 400°F, 200°C or Gas Mark 6 for 20 to 25 minutes until golden brown.
6. Remove from the oven and serve at once on a warm plate.

Serving Suggestion
Try serving with a tomato salad and a whole a wheat roll.

Chestnuts with Rice

1	Cup	Sliced Mushroom
1	Cup	Sliced Onion
3	Cups	Boiled Chestnuts
1	Tablespoon	Butter
1	Tablespoon	White Plain Flour
1	Pinch	Salt & Pepper
½		Vegetable Stock Cube
1	Cup	Water
1	Cup	White Wine
2	Cup	Cooked Rice

1. Sauté the onion and mushrooms in the butter until they are brown.
2. Add the flour and blend it in well.
3. Mix stock cube with the water then gradually add stock to saucepan.
4. Peel and chop the chestnuts and add to saucepan mix well.
5. Add the seasoning and the white wine.
6. Bring just to boiling point then remove from heat and serve over the cooked rice

Chicken Burgers

2	Cups	Minced Chicken
1	Cup	Fresh White Breadcrumbs
1	Small	Finely Chopped Onion
1	Teaspoon	Dried Mix Herbs
1	Teaspoon	Tomato Puree

1. In a bowl, mix the onion, chicken, breadcrumbs, herbs and tomato puree.
2. Divide the mixture to make two burgers and pat these in to two round shapes.
3. Grill or fry burgers for 10 to 12 minutes turning once.
4. Serve with relish and salad in burger buns.

Christmas Chicken Crackers

4	Tablespoons	Butter
1	Clove	Garlic, crushed
1	Teaspoon	Lime Juice
1	Teaspoon	Light Soy Sauce
1	Cup	Bean Sprouts, washed
¼	Teaspoon	Brown Sugar
2	Tablespoons	Tomato Ketchup
1	Cup	Cooked Chicken
2	Sheets	Filo Pastry
3	Cups	Cooking Oil

1. Place a wok or a deep frying pan over a moderate heat, add 1 tablespoon of butter and melt it.
2. Add the crushed garlic to the frying pan and sauté for 3 to 4 minutes.
3. Add the limejuice, soy sauce, bean sprouts, brown sugar, tomato ketchup and the chickens to the pan, stirring well and cook for 1 to 2 minutes.
4. Take the sheets of filo and lay them flat and brush with the butter and fold them in half-length ways.
5. Now place half of the warm mixture in the middle of each of the long edges of filo and roll up.
6. Twist the ends of the filo rolls where there is no filling to form a cracker shape.
7. Return to wok or frying pan to the heat and add the oil, place the filo crackers in the oil and cook for 4 to 5 minutes or until filo is brown.
8. Remove from oil and place on kitchen paper to drain.

Crepes with Curried Tuna

1½	Cups	SR Flour White
1	Cup	Milk
½	Cup	Water
1	Tablespoon	Sugar
2	Tablespoons	Vegetable Oil
1	Large	Egg
1	Small Tin	Tuna in a Curry Sauce
1	Cup	Cheddar Cheese, grated

1. Add the flour, water, milk, egg and sugar into a mixing bowl and blend on high speed for 1 minute with an electric mixer or for 5 minutes with a hand balloon whisk
2. Refrigerate mixture for 2 hours or overnight.
3. Place a 6" frying pan or omelette pan over a medium heat brush the bottom and sides of pan with the vegetable oil.
4. Then pour in ¼ cup of the batter into the pan; tipping pan to coat bottom with batter then using spatula gently pull it away from edge of pan.
5. Cook until top is just set and bottom is lightly browned then with a spatula, turn the crepe over and cook the other side for about 1 minute.
6. Repeat the procedure until all batter is used.
7. Open tuna and stir it then place a small amount in the centre of each crepe.
8. Fold the crepes and place in an ovenproof dish.
9. Sprinkle the grated cheddar cheese over the top.
10. Bake in a moderate oven at 350°F, 180°C or Gas Mark 4 for 5 minutes until cheese melts.

Crepes with Tuna Garlic and Herbs

1½	Cups	SR Flour White
1	Cup	Milk
½	Cup	Water
1	Tablespoon	Sugar
2	Tablespoons	Vegetable Oil
1	Large	Egg
1	Small Tin	Tuna with Mayonnaise Garlic & Herbs
1	Cup	Cheddar Cheese, grated

1. Add the flour, water, milk, egg and sugar into a mixing bowl and blend on high speed for 1 minute with an electric mixer or for 5 minutes with a hand balloon whisk
2. Refrigerate mixture for 2 hours or overnight.
3. Place a 6" frying pan or omelette pan over a medium heat brush the bottom and sides of pan with the vegetable oil.
4. Then pour in ¼ cup of the batter into the pan; tipping pan to coat bottom with batter then using spatula gently pull it away from edge of pan.
5. Cook until top is just set and bottom is lightly browned then with a spatula, turn the crepe over and cook the other side for about 1 minute.
6. Repeat the procedure until all batter is used.
7. Open tuna and stir it then place a small amount in the centre of each crepe.
8. Fold the crepes and place in an ovenproof dish.
9. Sprinkle the grated cheddar cheese over the top.
10. Bake in a moderate oven at 350°F, 180°C or Gas Mark 4 for 5 minutes until cheese melts.

Deep Dish Pepper & Mushroom Pizza

1	Cup	SR Flour
2	Tablespoons	Extra Virgin Olive Oil
1	Tablespoon	Water
1	Teaspoon	Salt
1	Small Tin	Tomatoes, chopped
1	Cup	Mozzarella Cheese, grated
1	Small	Yellow Pepper, finely chopped
1	Cup	Mushrooms, chopped
1	Teaspoon	Italian Seasoning

1. In a bowl mix the flour, salt, water and oil into a stiff dough.
2. Roll out the dough on a floured surface into a circle.
3. Line the base and sides of a greased small Yorkshire pudding tin.
4. Heat a pan over moderate heat and add tomatoes, chopped pepper and herbs bring to the boil and let boil for 5 to 7 minutes until the sauce has reduced by half.
5. Pour over base and top with mushrooms and the cheese.
6. Bake in a moderate oven at 400°F, 200°C or Gas Mark 6 for 15 to 20 minutes until golden brown.
7. Remove from the oven and eat at once.

Fish Kebabs

1	Medium	Fish Steak, cubed
1	Medium	Red Pepper, cubed
8	Small	Button Mushrooms
2	Tablespoons	Natural Yoghurt
1	Teaspoon	Pasanda Curry Paste
1	Pinch	Salt & Pepper
2	Cloves	Garlic, crushed

1. Place cubed fish, mushrooms and peppers in to a bowl with the honey, yoghurt, garlic, seasoning and curry paste mix together.
2. Assemble kebab by pushing fish onto skewers alternating with the peppers and mushrooms.
3. Cook under a hot grill for 12 to 14 minutes turning frequently.
4. To serve place on a bed of rice.

Garlic Oven Chips

2	Medium	Potatoes, peeled and cut into chips
1	Tablespoon	Cooking Oil
1	Teaspoon	Garlic Powder
1	Large	Plastic |Food Bag

1. Preheat an oven to 220°C, 425°F or Gas Mark 7.
2. Place a saucepan of salt water over a moderate heat and bring to the boil, when boiling place the chipped potatoes in the saucepan and boil for 4 to 5 minutes only.
3. Remove the saucepan from the heat and empty chipped potatoes into colander then place on kitchen paper to drain well and cool.
4. Add garlic powder to a large plastic food bag then add chipped potatoes close the top of bag and shake well.
5. Open the bag and pour the oil into it then add chipped potatoes close the bag again and shake well.
6. Open the bag and empty onto the baking sheet.
7. Bake for 30 to 35 minutes turning during the cooking time.

Italian Beef Strudel

1	Small Tin	Chopped Tomatoes
2	Cups	Lean Minced Beef
2	Sheets	Filo Pastry
2	Cloves	Garlic, crushed
1	Small	Onion, finely chopped
2	Tablespoons	Mozzarella Cheese, grated
1	Teaspoon	Tomato Puree
1	Teaspoon	Italian Seasoning
1	Tablespoon	Butter
1	Pinch	Salt & Pepper
1	Tablespoon	Extra Virgin Olive Oil

1. Heat a frying pan over a moderate heat add beef, onions and garlic, stir until meat browns and separates into grains.
2. Add chopped tomatoes, tomato puree, Italian seasoning, salt and pepper.
3. Bring to the boil then reduce heat stir from time to time.
4. Cook for about 14 to 18 minutes until sauce thickens.
5. Lay flat one of the sheets of filo pastry and brush with oil then sprinkle with the mozzarella cheese
6. Now brush the other sheet with oil and place over the top of the cheese.
7. Spread the sauce mixture over the pastry leaving a gap all around the edges.
8. Fold in the short end and roll up.
9. Transfer to an oiled baking sheet
10. Bake in a moderate oven at 375°F, 190 °C or Gas Mark 5 for 15 to 20 minutes till golden brown.

Italian Tomato Bake

1	Slice	White Bread, diced
1	Large	Plastic Food Bag
1	teaspoon	Garlic Powder
1	Large	Tomato, thinly sliced
½	Cup	Emmental Cheese, grated
½	Cup	Mozzarella Cheese, grated
1	Tablespoon	Basil
2	Tablespoons	Virgin Olive Oil

1. Preheat an oven to 200°C, 400°F or Gas Mark 6.
2. Place diced bread in the plastic bag add garlic powder close top and shake well.
3. Open bag and add 1 tablespoon of the oil close top and shake well.
4. Empty on to a baking sheet and place in the oven cook for 8 to 9 minutes then remove and keep warm.
5. Lay half of the sliced tomato on the base of an individual casserole dish and sprinkle with half of the remaining oil.
6. Sprinkle the emmental cheese over the tomatoes.
7. Cover with the rest of the tomatoes and sprinkle the rest of the remaining oil over the top.
8. Sprinkle the mozzarella cheese on top.
9. Bake at 200°C, 400°F or Gas Mark 6 for 9 to 10 minutes.
10. Remove from oven place on a serving plate and sprinkle with the croûtons.

Macaroni Cheese

½	Cup	Quick-Cook Macaroni
1	Tablespoon	Butter
½	Cup	Cheddar Cheese, grated
1	Dash	Worcestershire Sauce

1. Cook macaroni according to package instructions.
2. Drain and return to pot.
3. Add butter and stir until melted over a low heat.
4. Then add cheese, stirring it constantly, until cheese melts.
5. Season with a dash of worcestershire sauce.
6. Serve at once.

Microwave Salmon Steaks

1	Portion	Salmon Steak
1	Tablespoon	Soft Butter
1	Teaspoon	Lime Juice
½	Teaspoon	Dill Weed
1	Pinch	Paprika

1. Place the steak in microwave baking dish and brush with the soft butter sprinkle with limejuice and dill weed.
2. Cover, microwave on high power for 4-5 minutes.
3. When fish is cooked it will flake easily with a fork.
4. To serve place fish on a warm plate and pour over sauce then add a sprinkle of paprika if desired.

Mushroom Soufflé

½	Small Tin	Mushrooms, sliced
½	Small Tin	Condensed Mushroom Soup
1	Large	Egg
1	Pinch	Salt & Pepper

1. Grease a small soufflé dish and empty in the mushrooms
2. Separate the egg.
3. Empty the mushroom soup into a bowl and add the egg yolk, salt and pepper and mix together well.
4. Then whisk the egg white until it is stiff fold into egg yolk mixture.
5. Pour over mushrooms and bake at 400°F, 200°C or Gas Mark 6 for 20 to 25 minutes until golden brown.

Oven Chips

2	Medium	Potatoes, peeled and cut into chips
1	Tablespoon	Cooking Oil
1	Large	Plastic Food Bag

1. Preheat an oven to 220°C, 425°F or Gas Mark 7.
2. Place a saucepan of salt water over a moderate heat and bring to the boil when boiling place the chipped potatoes in the saucepan and boil for 4 to 5 minutes only.
3. Remove the saucepan from the heat and empty chipped potatoes into colander then place on kitchen paper to drain well and cool.
4. Pour oil into a large plastic food bag then add chipped potatoes close the top of bag and shake well.
5. Open the bag and empty onto the baking sheet.
6. Bake for 30 to 35 minutes turning during the cooking time.

Pork Sausage Toad in the Hole

2	Thick	Pork Sausages
½	Cup	SR Flour White
½	Cup	Milk
1	Small	Egg
1	Tablespoon	Vegetable Oil

1. Preheat oven at 425°F, 220°C or Gas Mark 7
2. In a bowl mix the flour, salt, egg and milk until smooth.
3. Use oil to grease two individual Yorkshire pudding tins.
4. Place a sausage in each tin and pick it well.
5. Put tins in oven for about 9 to 10 until the sausages are beginning to brown.
6. Remove from oven and pour over each sausage the batter mix, return to the oven for about 20 to 25 minutes.
7. Serving Suggestion
8. Serve with gravy, mashed potatoes and a green vegetable.

Potato Skins with Cajun Dip

1	Medium	Baking Potato
½	Cup	Natural Yoghurt
1	Teaspoon	Tomato Puree
1	Tablespoon	Cajun Spice

1. Preheat oven to 400°F, 200°C or Gas Mark 6
2. Wash potato and cook for about 40 minutes or until cooked.
3. When cooked halve baked potato lengthwise and scoop out pulp, leaving some pulp attached to skin try to avoid breaking the skin.
4. Cut potato skins into quarters and place on grill skin-sides down grill for 5 minutes or until crisp.
5. Mix the yoghurt and Cajun spice place in a ramekin dish and serve with potato skins

Sauté Shrimps & Mushrooms

1	Tablespoons	Butter.
2	Cloves	Garlic, crushed.
1	Cup	Mushroom, chopped.
1	Cup	Cooked Shrimps.
1	Slice	White Bread
1	Pinch	Paprika

1. Place a frying pan over a moderate heat, add the butter and melt it.
2. Add the crushed garlic and mushrooms to the frying pan and sauté for 3 to 4 minutes.
3. Remove the crusts from the slice of white bread and roll it flat with a roiling pin.
4. Toast the bread on both sides until it is a light golden colour.
5. Add the shrimps to the frying pan and stirring well for 1 to 2 minutes just to warm the shrimps through.
6. Place the toasted bread on a warm plate, and top with the shrimps and garlic mixture then sprinkle with paprika.

Shrimps on Toast

1	Slice	Thick White Bread
½	Cup	Cooked Peeled Shrimps
2	Tablespoons	Butter
¼	Teaspoon	Paprika
¼	Teaspoon	Chilli Powder
¼	Teaspoon	Cumin

1. Remove the crust from the bread and roll out with a rolling pin then cut in half length ways.
2. Butter bread on both sides with 1 tablespoon of the butter and place on a baking sheet.
3. Bake in a moderate oven at 350°F, 180°C or Gas Mark 4 for 12 to 14 minutes until golden brown.
4. Melt the other tablespoon of butter in a saucepan over a medium heat; add the shrimps and spices, stir well.
5. Heat for 2 to 3 minutes and then spoon on top of the toast.

Stuffed Peppers

1	Small	Red Pepper
1	Small	Yellow Pepper
1	Small	Green Pepper
2	Cups	Cooked Mixed Vegetable Rice, frozen
1	Tablespoon	Butter
1	Pinch	Salt & Pepper

1. Wipe the peppers with kitchen paper then remove the top carefully, keep and replace later.
2. Now with a spoon carefully scoop out the seeds.
3. Place the defrosted rice in a bowl add the salt, pepper and butter and mix well.
4. Spoon the mixture into the peppers and place the tops back on.
5. Place on a baking sheet and cook in a moderate 160°C, 325°F or Gas Mark 3 for 18 to 20 minutes.

Swiss Eggs

2	Large	Eggs
1	Tablespoon	Butter, grated
1	Tablespoon	Parmesan cheese, grated
1	Tablespoon	Double Cream
1	Tablespoon	Gruyere Cheese, grated
1	Pinch	Parmesan Cheese

1. Butter two ramekins dishes.
2. Break an egg carefully into each cup.
3. Sprinkle with salt and pepper to taste.
4. Pour 1 tablespoon of cream over each egg.
5. Dot eggs with butter and sprinkle with the cheese and pour over cream.
6. Set the ramekins dishes into a baking tin.
7. Now add enough boiling water into baking tin to come half way up the sides of the dishes.
8. Bake in a moderate oven at 350°F, 180°C or Gas Mark 4 for 10 minutes.

Tuna Lasagne with Sweetcorn

2	Sheets	No Pre-Cooking Lasagne
1	Small Tin	Tomatoes, chopped
2	Cups	Milk
1	Small Tin	Tuna with Mayonnaise & Sweetcorn
2	Cloves	Garlic, grated
1	Small	Onion, finely chopped
2	Tablespoons	Mozzarella Cheese, grated
1	Teaspoon	Tomato Puree
1	Teaspoon	Italian Seasoning
1	Tablespoon	Butter
1	Tablespoon	Cornflour

1. Heat a frying pan over a moderate heat; add the onions, garlic and sauté for 4 minutes.
2. Add chopped tomatoes, tomato puree, tuna and Italian seasoning.
3. Bring to the boil then reduce heat stir from time to time.
4. Cook for about 14 to 18 minutes until sauce thickens.
5. Put half of the mixture into a shallow ovenproof dish cover with a sheet of lasagne then the remaining sauces and top with a sheet of lasagne.
6. Place a saucepan over a medium heat add the butter and melt then add the cornflour and cook for 1 to 2 minutes.
7. Slowly add the milk, salt and pepper, stir well and increase the heat and cook for 4 minutes until sauce thickens.
8. Pour over the top of the last sheet of lasagne and sprinkle with the mozzarella cheese.
9. Bake in a moderate oven at 375°F, 190 °C or Gas Mark 5 for 25 to 30 minutes till golden brown.

Tuna Pizza

1	Cup	SR Flour White
2	Tablespoons	Extra Virgin Olive Oil
1	Tablespoon	Water
1	Teaspoon	Salt
1	Small Tin	Tomatoes, chopped
1	Cup	Cheese, grated
1	Small Tin	Tuna, drained and chopped
1	Teaspoon	Italian Seasoning

1. In a bowl mix the flour, salt, water and oil to a stiff dough.
2. Roll out the dough on a floured surface into a circle.
3. Then place onto a greased baking sheet.
4. Heat a pan over moderate heat and add tomatoes and herbs bring to the boil and let boil for 5 to 7 minutes until the sauce has reduced by half.
5. Pour over base and top with tuna and the cheese.
6. Bake in a moderate oven at 400°F, 200°C or Gas Mark 6 for 15 to 20 minutes till golden brown.

Vegetarian Sausage Toad in the Hole

2	Thick	Vegetarian Sausages
½	Cup	SR Flour White
½	Cup	Milk
1	Small	Egg
1	Tablespoon	Vegetable Oil

1. Preheat oven at 425°F, 220°C or Gas Mark 7
2. In a bowl mix the flour, salt, egg and milk until smooth.
3. Use oil to grease two individual Yorkshire pudding tins.
4. Place a sausage in each tin and pick it well.
5. Put tins in oven for about 9 to 10 minutes until the sausages are beginning to brown.
6. Remove from oven and pour the batter mix over each sausage, return to the oven for about 20 to 25 minutes.

Serving Suggestion
Serve with gravy, mashed potatoes and a green vegetable.

INDEX

A
A Toasted Breakfast · 47
Al-Badinjan · 173
Almond & Dark Chocolate Mousse · 131
Almond & White Chocolate Mousse · 132
Almond Stuffed Dates with Bacon · 5
Almond Stuffed Dates with Smokey Bacon · 174
Almonds
  Almond Stuffed Dates with Bacon · 5
  Almond Stuffed Dates with Smokey Bacon · 174
  Avocado Almonds & Mozzarella Tempura · 176
  Avocado Almonds Tempura · 10
Antipasto · 6
Apple
  Apple & Leek Soup · 8
  Apple & Potato Bake · 175
  Apple & Stilton Crumble · 134
  Apple and Cheddar Cheese Crumble · 133
  Apple and Cheese Toast · 7
  Breakfast Apple & Banana Bars · 58
  Breakfast Apple & Walnut Bars · 59
Apple & Potato Bake · 175
Apple & Stilton Crumble · 134
Apple and Cheddar Cheese Crumble · 133
Apple and Cheese Toast · 7
Apricot
  Sorbet · 135
Apricot Sorbet · 135

Artichoke
  Artichoke Hearts and Parma · 9
Artichoke Hearts and Parma · 9
Aubergine
  Al-Badinjan · 173
  Cajun Al-Badinjan · 183
Avocado
  Avocado Almonds & Mozzarella Tempura · 176
  Avocado Almonds Tempura · 10
  Avocado Walnuts & Gloucester Tempura · 12
  Soup · 11
Avocado Almonds & Mozzarella Tempura · 176
Avocado Almonds Tempura · 10
Avocado Soup · 11
Avocado Walnuts & Gloucester Tempura · 12

B
Baby Pineapple Boats · 13
Bacon
  Almond Stuffed Dates with Bacon · 5
  Almond Stuffed Dates with Smokey Bacon · 174
  Bacon Folded Omelette · 54
  Feta & Bacon Folded Omelette · 30
  Mozzarella & Bacon Folded Omelette · 71
Bacon & Cheese Bagel · 48
Bacon & Cheese Cheese-Crumpet · 49
Bacon & Cheese Croissant · 50
Bacon & Cheese with Garlic Croissant · 51
Bacon & Cheese with Ham Bagel · 52

Bacon & Cheese with Herbs Croissant · 53
Bacon Folded Omelette · 54
Bagels
  Bacon & Cheese · 48
  Bacon & Cheese with Ham · 52
Baked Alaska · 136
Baked Apple with Calvados · 137
Baked Apple with Whisky · 138
Baked Cajun Fish · 177
Baked Eggs with Ham & Potato · 55
Baked French Toast · 14
Baked Green & Yellow Pepper Wedges · 15
Baked Lemon Pudding · 139
Baked Onion · 178
Baked Orange Pudding · 140
Baked Potato Spears · 17
Banana
  Banana & Pear Breakfast Shake · 56
  Banana Breakfast Shake · 57
  Breakfast Apple & Banana Bars · 58
  Breakfast Banana & Walnut Bars · 61
  Pudding · 141
Banana & Pear Breakfast Shake · 56
Banana Breakfast Shake · 57
Banana Pudding · 141
Banana Sorbet · 142
Barbecue Baby Ribs · 89
Barbecue Chicken Drumsticks · 90
Barbecue Pork Chop · 91
Basic Crepes · 143
Beans

Cajun Black Eye Beans & Rice · 184
Cajun Red Beans & Rice · 100
Beef
  Beef & Pineapple Salad · 93
  Beefsteak with Mushroom & Onion Gravy · 97
  Bolognese · 98
  Burgers Italian · 179
  Chop Suey · 94
  Curry · 95
  Italian Beef Strudel · 198
  Lasagne · 92
  Risotto · 180
  Stroganoff · 96
Beef & Pineapple Salad · 93
Beef Burgers Italian · 179
Beef Chop Suey · 94
Beef Curry · 95
Beef Lasagne · 92
Beef Risotto · 180
Beef Stroganoff · 96
Beefsteak with Mushroom & Onion Gravy · 97
Black Eye Beans Italian · 181
Blue Cheese & Walnut Dip · 18
Bolognese · 98
Bread
  Gloucester Cheese Stuffed · 66
  Stilton Cheese Stuffed · 43
Bread & Butter Pudding with Golden Syrup · 145
Bread & Butter Pudding with Honey · 146
Bread and Butter Pudding · 144
Breakfast Apple & Banana Bars · 58
Breakfast Apple & Walnut Bars · 59
Breakfast Banana & Walnut Bars · 61
Breakfast Cherry Bars · 62

Breakfasts
   Ploughmen's · 75
Broccoli
   Broccoli & Cheddar Soup · 19
   Lasagne · 182
Broccoli Lasagne · 182

C

Cajun
   Al-Badinjan · 183
   Baked Cajun Fish · 177
   Black Eye Beans & Rice · 184
   Potato Skins with Cajun Dip · 205
   Red Beans & Rice · 100
Cajun Al-Badinjan · 183
Cajun Black Eye Beans & Rice · 184
Cajun Chicken Breast · 99
Cajun Red Beans & Rice · 100
Carrot
   Carrot & Orange Soup · 20
   Carrot & Potato Soup · 21
   Carrot & Turnip Soup · 185
Carrot & Orange Soup · 20
Carrot & Potato Soup · 21
Carrot & Turnip Soup · 185
Cauliflower & Broccoli Soup · 22
Celery
   Soufflé · 186
Celery & Green Pepper Soup · 23
Celery & Parsnip Soup · 24
Celery Soufflé · 186
Cheddar Stuffed Brown Pasta Shells · 187
Cheese & Mushroom Pizza · 188
Cheese & Mushroom Rolls · 25
Cheese & Pineapple Pizza · 101
Cheese & Pineapple Soufflé · 189

Cheese Dishes
   Apple & Stilton Crumble · 134
   Apple and Cheddar Cheese Crumble · 133
   Apple and Cheese Toast · 7
   Artichoke Hearts and Parma · 9
   Avocado Almonds & Mozzarella Tempura · 176
   Avocado Almonds Tempura · 10
   Avocado Walnuts & Gloucester Tempura · 12
   Bacon & Cheese Bagel · 48
   Bacon & Cheese Cheese-Crumpet · 49
   Bacon & Cheese Croissant · 50
   Blue Cheese & Walnut Dip · 18
   Cheddar
      Broccoli & Cheddar Soup · 19
   Cheddar Stuffed Brown Pasta Shells · 187
   Cheese & Mushroom Pizza · 188
   Cheese & Mushroom Rolls · 25
   Cheese Stuffed Plantains · 102
   Cream Cheese Omelette · 63
   Deep Dish Pineapple & Ham Cheese Pizza · 111
   Edam Stuffed Brown Pasta Quills · 114
   Fried Brie Cheese · 32
   Fried Quark Cheese · 33
   Gloucester Cheese Stuffed Bread · 66
   Grapefruit and Stilton Surprise · 35
   Italian Tomato Bake · 199
   Macaroni Cheese · 200
   Mozzarella & Bacon Folded Omelette · 71

Nectarine & Cheese Crumble · 162
Pear & Cheese Toast · 73
Plaice with Cheese Sauce · 124
Scottish Rarebit · 79
Stilton Cheese Stuffed Bread · 43
Swiss Eggs · 209
Turkey & Cheese Croissant · 84
Cheese Stuffed Plantains · 102
Cheesecake
  Cherry · 147
  Lemon · 157
Cheese-Crumpets
  Bacon & Cheese · 49
Cherry
  Breakfast Bars · 62
Cherry Cheesecake · 147
Chestnuts with Rice · 190
Chicken
  Barbecue Chicken Drumsticks · 90
  Burgers · 191
  Cajun Chicken Breast · 99
  Chicken & Pineapple Salad · 26
  Chicken & Sweetcorn Soup · 27
  Chicken Chop Suey · 103
  Christmas Chicken Crackers · 192
  Curry · 104
  Goujons Chicken · 116
  with Mushrooms & Whisky · 105
Chicken & Pineapple Salad · 26
Chicken Burgers · 191
Chicken Chop Suey · 103
Chicken Curry · 104
Chicken with Mushrooms & Whisky · 105
Chilli Con Carne · 107

Chinese Folded Omelette · 106
Chocolate Crepes · 148
Chocolate Egg Custard · 149
Chocolate Pizza · 150
Chop Suey
  Beef · 94
  Chicken · 103
  Prawn · 125
Christmas Chestnut Pie · 108
Christmas Chicken Crackers · 192
Cod
  Grilled with a Whisky Sauce · 118
  with Cheese Sauce · 110
Cod Parcels · 109
Cod with Cheese Sauce · 110
Complete Breakfast · 82
Crab
  Crab & Sweetcorn Soup · 28
Cream Cheese Omelette · 63
Crepes
  Basic · 143
  Blackcurrants and Ice Cream · 151
  Chocolate · 148
  Curried Tuna · 193
  Raspberries & Ice Cream · 152
  Strawberries & Ice Cream · 153
  Tuna Garlic and Herbs · 194
Crepes with Blackcurrants and Ice Cream · 151
Crepes with Curried Tuna · 193
Crepes with Raspberries & Ice Cream · 152
Crepes with Strawberries & Ice Cream · 153
Crepes with Tuna Garlic and Herbs · 194
Croissant

Turkey & Cheese Croissant · 84
Croissants
    Bacon & Cheese · 50
    Bacon & Cheese with Garlic · 51
    Bacon & Cheese with Herbs · 53
Croûtons
    Garlic Croûtons · 34
Crumble
    Apple & Stilton · 134
    Apple and Cheddar Cheese · 133
    Italian Lamb · 122
    Nectarine & Cheese · 162
    Spiced Peach · 167
Currant Steamed Pudding · 154
Curry
    Beef · 95
    Chicken · 104

D

Dates
    Almond Stuffed Dates with Bacon · 5
    Almond Stuffed Dates with Smokey Bacon · 174
Deep Dish Pepper & Mushroom Pizza · 195
Deep Dish Pineapple & Ham Cheese Pizza · 111
Deep Fried Garlic Mushrooms · 29
Dips
    Blue Cheese & Walnut Dip · 18
    Cajun
        Potato Skins with Cajun Dip · 205
    Potato Skins with Cucumber Dip · 40
    Potato Skins with Garlic · 41

Drinks
    Banana Breakfast Shake · 57
    Pineapple Delight · 164
    Strawberry Delight · 169
Duck
    Duck with Orange · 113
    with Blackcurrants · 112
Duck with Blackcurrants · 112
Duck with Orange · 113

E

Edam Stuffed Brown Pasta Quills · 114
Egg Custard · 155
Egg Dishes
    Chinese Folded Omelette · 106
    Feta & Bacon Folded Omelette · 30
Eggs
    Baked Eggs with Ham & Potato · 55
    Cream Cheese Omelette · 63
    Eggs Florentine · 64
    Mozzarella & Bacon Folded Omelette · 71
    Scrambled Egg Pockets · 80
    Swiss Eggs · 209
    Tomato Folded Omelette · 83
Eggs Florentine · 64

F

Feta & Bacon Folded Omelette · 30
Fish Dishes
    Antipasto · 6
    Baked Cajun Fish · 177
    Cod Parcels · 109
    Cod with Cheese Sauce · 110
    Fish Kebabs · 196
    Grilled Cod with a Whisky Sauce · 118
    Grilled Salmon with a Schnapps Sauce · 120

Halibut with Cheese Sauce · 121
Jugged Kipper · 69
Microwave Salmon Steaks · 201
Scottish Rarebit · 79
Smoked Haddock on Toast · 81
Tuna Lasagne with Sweetcorn · 210
Tuna Pizza · 211
Fish Kebabs · 196
French Red Onion Soup · 31
French Toast · 65
Fried Brie Cheese · 32
Fried Quark Cheese · 33
Fruit
   Currant Steamed Pudding · 154
Fruit Steamed Pudding · 156

G

Gammon Steak with Pineapple Sauce · 115
Garlic Croûtons · 34
Garlic Oven Chips · 197
Gloucester Cheese Stuffed Bread · 66
Goujons Chicken · 116
Goujons Turkey · 117
Grapefruit
   Grapefruit and Stilton Surprise · 35
   Grapefruit Surprise · 67
   Pink Grapefruit Surprise · 74
Grapefruit and Stilton Surprise · 35
Grapefruit Surprise · 67
Green Pepper
   Celery & Green Pepper Soup · 23
Grilled Cod with a Whisky Sauce · 118
Grilled Lamb Chop with Mustard · 119
Grilled Salmon with a Schnapps Sauce · 120

H

Halibut with Cheese Sauce · 121
Ham
   Deep Dish Pineapple & Ham Cheese Pizza · 111
   Ham & Pineapple Salad · 36
   Parma Ham & Pineapple · 72
   Prosciutto Ham & Mixed Fruit · 77
Ham & Pineapple Salad · 36
Hot Scrambled Eggs · 68

I

Italian Beef Strudel · 198
Italian Lamb Crumble · 122
Italian Tomato Bake · 199

J

Jugged Kipper · 69

K

Kebabs
   Fish · 196
Kipper
   Jugged · 69

L

Lamb
   Barbecue Pork Chop · 91
   Grilled Lamb Chop with Mustard · 119
   Hotpot · 123
   Italian Lamb Crumble · 122
Lamb Hotpot · 123
Lasagne
   Beef · 92
   Broccoli · 182
   Tuna with Sweetcorn · 210
Leek

Apple & Leek Soup · 8
Leek & Potato Soup · 37
Leek & Potato Soup · 37
Lemon
  Baked Lemon Pudding · 139
Lemon Cheesecake · 157

M

Macaroni Cheese · 200
Malt Bread & Butter Pudding · 158
Malt French Toast · 70
Mango
  Sorbet · 160
Mango Cloud · 159
Mango Sorbet · 160
Microwave Salmon Steaks · 201
Mincemeat Parcels · 161
Minestrone Soup · 38
Mousse
  Almond & Dark Chocolate · 131
  Almond & White Chocolate · 132
Mozzarella & Bacon Folded Omelette · 71
Mushroom
  Beefsteak with Mushroom & Onion Gravy · 97
Mushroom Soufflé · 202
Mushrooms
  Cheese & Mushroom Pizza · 188
  Cheese & Mushroom Rolls · 25
  Deep Fried Garlic · 29
  Sauté Prawns & Mushrooms · 42
  Sauté Shrimps & Mushrooms · 206
  Steak & Mushroom Pie · 127
  Steak with Mushrooms & Schnapps · 128

N

Nectarine & Cheese Crumble · 162
Nuts
  Christmas Chestnut Pie · 108

O

Omelette
  Bacon Folded Omelette · 54
Orange
  Baked Orange Pudding · 140
  Carrot & Orange Soup · 20
Orange Egg Custard · 163
Oven Chips · 203

P

Parma Ham & Pineapple · 72
Parsnip
  Celery & Parsnip Soup · 24
Pasta Dishes
  Cheddar Stuffed Brown Pasta Shells · 187
  Edam Stuffed Brown Pasta Quills · 114
Peach
  Spiced Peach Crumble · 167
Pear
  Pear & Cheese Toast · 73
Pear & Cheese Toast · 73
Peppers
  Green
    Baked Green & Yellow Pepper Wedges · 15
  Stuffed · 208
  Yellow
    Baked Green & Yellow Pepper Wedges · 15
Pies
  Christmas Chestnut · 108
  Steak & Mushroom · 127
Pineapple
  Baby Pineapple Boats · 13
  Beef & Pineapple Salad · 93

Chicken & Pineapple Salad · 26
Deep Dish Pineapple & Ham Cheese Pizza · 111
Ham & Pineapple Salad · 36
Parma Ham & Pineapple · 72
Pineapple Delight · 164
Pineapple Delight · 164
Pink Grapefruit Surprise · 74
Pizza
  Cheese & Mushroom · 188
  Cheese & Pineapple · 101
  Chocolate · 150
  Deep Dish Pepper & Mushroom Pizza · 195
  Tuna · 211
Plaice
  with Cheese Sauce · 124
Plaice with Cheese Sauce · 124
Ploughmen's Breakfast · 75
Pork
  Barbecue Baby Ribs · 89
Pork Sausage Toad in the Hole · 204
Potato
  Apple & Potato Bake · 175
  Baked Eggs with Ham & Potato · 55
  Baked Potato Soup · 16
  Baked Potato Spears · 17
  Carrot & Potato Soup · 21
  Leek & Potato Soup · 37
  Potato Skins with Cajun Dip · 205
  Potato Skins with Garlic Dip · 41
Potato Skins with Cucumber Dip · 40
Potato Skins with Garlic Dip · 41
Prawn
  Chop Suey · 125
Prawn Chop Suey · 125
Prawns
  on Toast · 76
  Sauté · 126
  Sauté Prawns & Mushrooms · 42
Prawns on Toast · 76
Prosciutto Ham & Mixed Fruit · 77
Puddings
  Currant Steamed Pudding · 154
  Fruit Steamed Pudding · 156
  Malt Bread & Butter Pudding · 158

Q
Quick Kedgeree · 78

R
Raisin Steamed Pudding · 165
Raspberries
  Crepes with Raspberries & Ice Cream · 152
Raspberry Soufflé · 166
Rice
  Cajun Black Eye Beans & Rice · 184
  Chestnuts with Rice · 190
  Red Beans & Rice · 100
Risotto
  Beef · 180
Rolls
  Cheese & Mushroom · 25

S
Salad
  Beef & Pineapple · 93
  Chicken & Pineapple · 26
  Ham & Pineapple · 36
Salmon
  Grilled with a Schnapps Sauce · 120
  Microwave Salmon Steaks · 201
Sauté Prawns · 126

Sauté Prawns & Mushrooms · 42
Sauté Shrimps & Mushrooms · 206
Scottish Rarebit · 79
Scrambled Egg Pockets · 80
Seafood
    Baked Cajun Fish · 177
    Cod Parcels · 109
    Cod with Cheese Sauce · 110
    Crab & Sweetcorn Soup · 28
    Crepes with Curried Tuna · 193
    Crepes with Tuna Garlic and Herbs · 194
    Fish Kebabs · 196
    Grilled Cod with a Whisky Sauce · 118
    Halibut with Cheese Sauce · 121
    Jugged Kipper · 69
    Plaice with Cheese Sauce · 124
    Prawn Chop Suey · 125
    Prawns on Toast · 76
    Sauté Prawns · 126
    Sauté Prawns & Mushrooms · 42
    Sauté Shrimps & Mushrooms · 206
    Shrimps on Toast · 207
    Tuna Lasagne with Sweetcorn · 210
    Tuna Pizza · 211
Shakes
    Banana & Pear Breakfast Shake · 56
Shrimp
    Sauté Shrimps & Mushrooms · 206
    Shrimps on Toast · 207
    Shrimps on Toast · 207
Smoked Haddock
    Smoked Haddock on Toast · 81
    Smoked Haddock on Toast · 81

Sorbet
    Apricot · 135
    Banana · 142
    Mango · 160
Soufflés
    Celery · 186
    Cheese & Pineapple · 189
    Mushroom · 202
    Raspberry · 166
    Summer Fruits · 170
Soups
    Apple & Leek · 8
    Avocado · 11
    Baked Potato · 16
    Broccoli & Cheddar · 19
    Carrot & Orange · 20
    Carrot & Potato · 21
    Carrot & Turnip · 185
    Cauliflower & Broccoli · 22
    Celery & Green Pepper · 23
    Celery & Parsnip · 24
    Chicken & Sweetcorn · 27
    Crab & Sweetcorn · 28
    French Red Onion · 31
    Leek & Potato · 37
    Minestrone · 38
    Vegetable · 44
Spiced Peach Crumble · 167
Steak
    Steak & Mushroom Pie · 127
    Steak with Mushrooms & Schnapps · 128
    Steak & Mushroom Pie · 127
    Steak with Mushrooms & Schnapps · 128
Steaks
    Microwave Salmon · 201
    Stilton Cheese Stuffed Bread · 43
Strawberry
    Strawberry Delight · 169
    Strawberry Cloud · 168
    Strawberry Delight · 169

Stroganoff
    Beef · 96
Strudel
    Italian Beef · 198
Stuffed Peppers · 208
Summer Fruits Soufflé · 170
Sweetcorn
    Chicken & Sweetcorn Soup · 27
    Crab & Sweetcorn Soup · 28
Swiss Eggs · 209

T
Tempura
    Avocado Almonds · 10
    Avocado Almonds & Mozzarella · 176
    Avocado Walnuts & Gloucester · 12
The Complete Breakfast · 82
Toast
    Baked French Toast · 14
    French · 65
    Malt French Toast · 70
    Walnut French Toast · 85
    Whole-Wheat French Toast · 86
Tomato
    Folded Omelette · 83
    Italian Tomato Bake · 199
Tomato Folded Omelette · 83
Tuna
    Antipasto · 6

Crepes with Curried Tuna · 193
Crepes with Tuna Garlic and Herbs · 194
Lasagne with Sweetcorn · 210
Tuna Lasagne with Sweetcorn · 210
Tuna Pizza · 211
Turkey
    Goujons Turkey · 117
    Turkey & Cheese Croissant · 84
Turkey & Cheese Croissant · 84
Turnip
    Carrot & Turnip Soup · 185

V
Vegetable Soup · 44
Vegetarian Sausage Toad in the Hole · 212

W
Walnut
    Breakfast Apple & Walnut Bars · 59
    Breakfast Banana & Walnut Bars · 61
Walnut French Toast · 85
Walnuts
    Avocado Walnuts & Gloucester Tempura · 12
Whole-Wheat French Toast · 86